GOD'S REVOLUTION

POPE BENEDICT XVI

God's Revolution

World Youth Day and Other Cologne Talks

IGNATIUS PRESS   SAN FRANCISCO

Cover photographs:
Cologne Cathedral,
by Peter Ginter (gettyimages.com)
and
Pope Benedict XVI,
by Allesandra Benedetti (corbis.com)

Cover design by Riz Boncan Marsella

ISBN 978-1-58617-145-2 (H)
ISBN 1-58617-145-3 (H)
ISBN 978-1-58617-146-9 (P)
ISBN 1-58617-146-1 (P)
Library of Congress Control Number 2005934792

Printed in the United States of America ⊚

CONTENTS

Ecumenical Dialogue

Concluding Talks

INTRODUCTION

Anyone who attended the Twentieth World Youth Day can testify that, like the preceding one, it was a great experience of faith and of Christianity put into practice—great, then, not only because of the number and the enthusiasm of the participants, but more profoundly because of the authenticity of their prayer, the shared sense of belonging to Christ and to the Church, the generosity of their commitment, too, in putting up with the inevitable fatigue and discomforts, and finally because of the joy and the Christian maturity of so many young people.

This World Youth Day had a new point of reference: Benedict XVI. He has taken up "with trepidation but also with joy" this great legacy bequeathed to him by his Predecessor; he constantly harked back to him, arousing the enthusiasm of the young people, and he emphasized the fruitfulness of the "intuition", or, rather, the "inspiration" by which John Paul II had been able to understand young people, had had confidence in them and had urged them to be "courageous heralds of the Gospel and intrepid builders of the civilization of truth, love and peace".

At the same time, Benedict XVI, discreetly and in a certain sense involuntarily, yet for that very reason in a particularly effective and profound manner, stamped the Twentieth World Youth Day with his own personal style and especially his way of living out his relationship with Christ. He did this, specifically, by making Jesus Christ himself, the Eucharistic Lord, the center and protagonist of the event. He did this by being completely himself, in the simplicity and gentility of his gestures, in the Christian joy that radiates from his face. The

---

Introduction translated from Italian by Michael J. Miller.

young people immediately noticed this, and they fell in love with it: and so the same bond of love that had united them with John Paul II embraced Benedict XVI also, with a natural spontaneity that surprised many observers but that is clear evidence of the ability of young people to see in the person of the Pope the Successor of Peter and Vicar of Christ, which testifies also to the genuine character of the rapport that Benedict XVI unexpectedly managed to establish with them.

The special charism of the new Pontiff produced yet another result: from this World Youth Day, specifically from the twelve speeches given by Benedict XVI, sprang a presentation of the mystery of Christ and of its fundamental implications for the lives of believers, for the mission of the Church and for the future of humanity—an overview that is contained in this little book. It is a book that was certainly written by the Pope, and at certain points improvised by him in the course of the meetings, but it is also, somehow, a book written by the young people: or, more precisely, it is also the product of the special bond that already unites Benedict XVI to young people, the result of that "exchange of gifts" which took place between him and them during the World Youth Day. It is a little book that will be very effective as a guide to the heart of the mystery of the God who saves us, as a stimulus to faith, to prayer, to conversion of hearts and of lives, as a source of light in which to exercise the gift of right judgment on our society and on our time: a Christian inspiration for young people, but not only for young people.

It is easy to follow the main thread running through this little book; indeed, it is pointed out by the theme of the Twentieth World Youth Day: "We have come to worship him" (Mt 2:2). Everything that is written here leads us to adore the Child who is God, whose love transforms and renews us and the whole world. In other words, this book is first and foremost a prayer, just as prayer and adoration of Christ in the Eucharist were the keynote of the Twentieth World Youth Day. Radiating from this book, as from World Youth Day, is sheer joy over the beauty of the faith, over the beauty of Christ and of life in Christ.

What I have tried to accomplish in these introductory pages is simply to point out a similar recurring motif and the unity of the overall plan into which each one of the twelve talks by Benedict XVI fits. My work was easy, and probably superfluous, because the Pope's words have, in addition to vigor and depth, a splendid consistency and an extraordinary clarity.

In this brief presentation we should concentrate right away on the fundamental contents, expressed particularly in Marienfeld, at the Vigil on Saturday evening and in the homily at the Mass the following morning. In the talk that he gave to the young people from the riverboat on the Rhine, Benedict XVI had already noted the essential purpose of this World Youth Day: to come to contemplate, both personally and as a community, the face of God revealed in the infant lying in the manger, then to experience prayer as a dialogue with God, who we know loves us and whom we in turn wish to love. Therefore the Pope makes an insistent appeal to all the young people who have come to World Youth Day, even to the unbaptized and to unbelievers: "Open wide your hearts to God! Let yourselves be surprised by Christ! Let him have 'the right of free speech' during these days! Open the doors of your freedom to his merciful love! . . . May you have a liberating experience of the Church as the place where God's merciful love reaches out to all people."

The Magi, too, as the Pope explained at the Vigil in Marienfeld, when they arrived at the little house in Bethlehem, had to allow themselves to be surprised by God, whom they met in a poor infant: a God quite different from the one they imagined. They had to change their ideas about God and about man, in particular they had to understand that God's power and way of acting are different from those of men, especially the powerful of this world. God, indeed, does not compete with earthly forms of power, but instead he contrasts "the noisy and ostentatious power of this world with the defenseless power of love, which succumbs to death on the Cross and dies ever anew throughout history; yet it is this same love which constitutes the new divine intervention that opposes injustice and ushers in the Kingdom of God."

In the homily at the Sunday morning Mass, Benedict XVI developed this thought more profoundly, in a Eucharistic key. With the words pronounced over the bread and wine in the cenacle, Jesus anticipates his own death, "he accepts it in his heart, and he transforms it into an action of love." The Crucifixion, which is externally a brutal act of violence, thus becomes internally an act of love, of total self-giving. This is the substantial transformation, the only one that is capable of initiating a series of transformations, the final goal of which is the transformation of the world, until God is everything to everyone (cf. 1 Cor 15:28). This decisive act of love, indeed, transforms even death into love and thus overcomes it from within, making the Resurrection present in it.

Benedict XVI resorted here to a striking, contemporary image, that of "nuclear fission [induced] in the very heart of being", to suggest this interior explosion of good that conquers evil and that is the only thing that can start the chain reaction of transformations that truly change and renew the world. This is the true revolution that mankind has always needed and desired. In contrast, the common program of the revolutions of the twentieth century was to stop waiting for God to intervene and, instead, to take the future of the world completely into their own hands; these revolutions had to use force in order to make absolute what is only relative, so as to take a partial, human perspective as an absolute standard and guide. But absolutizing what is relative is the very essence of totalitarianism; it does not liberate man but robs him of his dignity and enslaves him.

The fundamental transformation that takes place when the bread and wine become the Body and Blood of Christ requires and produces, first of all, *our* transformation. This Body and this Blood, in fact, are given to us so that we might be transformed in turn: that is to say, we come to be united to Christ and to the Father and thus become capable of submitting ourselves to God so as to make him the measure of our lives, by an act that does not alienate us from ourselves, but frees us in accordance with the most intimate truth of our being. This is the full meaning of adoration, which formed the center of gravity of the Twentieth World Youth Day.

In the talk that he gave to the young people from the riverboat on the Rhine, Benedict XVI had already quoted the words from his homily on April 24, [2005,] with which he began his ministry as Supreme Pastor: "If we let Christ into our lives, we lose nothing, . . . absolutely nothing of what makes life free, beautiful and great. . . . Only in this friendship is the great potential of human existence truly revealed." And at the Vigil in Marienfeld he added: the only thing that can save the world is "a return to the living God, our Creator, the guarantor of our freedom, the guarantor of what is really good and true". Indeed, "what could ever save us apart from love?" And God, the God who reveals himself to us in Jesus Christ, is precisely eternal love.

In practice, however, it is necessary for Christ's "hour", his gift of himself for our sake, to become in fact our "hour" as well: this will happen "if we allow ourselves, through the celebration of the Eucharist, to be drawn into that process of transformation that the Lord intends to bring about". That is, if we consent to change ourselves, to learn God's ways, to enter into the loving dynamic of the Eucharist, even to the gift and loss of ourselves so that we might really find ourselves and "become men of truth, of justice, of goodness, of forgiveness, of mercy". Therefore the Eucharist must become the center of our lives and, practically speaking, must give direction and meaning to our Sunday, the Lord's day, the day on which creation began and also the day of redemption, the day of the feast that God himself prepares for us. With a love for the Eucharist we can also rediscover the Sacrament of Reconciliation, "in which the merciful goodness of God always allows us to make a fresh start in our lives".

All of this touches and involves everything that is most intimate and personal in each one of us, while at the same time it unifies us and puts us all together into action, as the Body of Christ which is the Church, not an anonymous collectivity, but as a communion of persons. Indeed, by eating the one bread and thus uniting ourselves intimately with the one Christ, we become one among ourselves also. Benedict XVI forcefully and very persuasively emphasized that it is useless and misleading to construct for oneself, as often happens today, a private God or a private Jesus, which can be convenient but which ultimately leaves us lonely. Christ and the Father are shown to us in Sacred Scripture and reveal that they are alive "in the great procession of the faithful called the Church".

Of course, there is much about the Church that can be criticized, and the Lord himself told us that she is a net with both good fish and bad fish, a field with grain and darnel, wheat and weeds. Therefore John Paul II, on the one hand, showed us the true face of the Church in the great number of saints and blessed that he proclaimed, and, on the other hand, he asked pardon for the wrong that has been done over the course of history through the words and deeds of members of the Church. But this very fact is consoling to us: indeed, in this way, despite all our faults and failings, we can hope to be among the followers of Jesus, who called sinners. The Church is like a human family, but at the same time she is "the great family of God, through which he establishes an overarching communion and unity that embraces every continent, culture and nation", as we see at the World Youth Day in Cologne, an arch that encompasses heaven and earth, the past, the present and the future. Therefore let us be glad to belong to this big family, to have brothers and sisters and friends throughout the world and especially to be walking together with Christ, the star that illumines history.

Pope Benedict made the mystery of the Church and of our own vocation as Christians more concrete by proposing the example and the witness of the saints: that long procession of men and women—known or unknown—who in their lives constantly sought God and through whom the Lord, throughout history and still today, has opened up the Gospel before us and turned over the pages. They are "the shining path" of God. Having learned from Christ to give themselves, they show us the way to be happy and truly human. They are the true reformers who so many times lifted history up out of the valley of darkness into which it is always in danger of sinking. By contemplating their lives, we learn concretely what it means to "adore".

On this basis, in the final part of the homily at the Sunday morning Mass in Marienfeld, Benedict XVI formulated a great call to mission: "Anyone who has discovered Christ must lead others to him. A great joy cannot be kept to oneself. It has to be passed on." This call becomes even more urgent, given "a strange forgetfulness of God" that exists today in vast areas of the world and that ends up causing dissatisfaction and frustration. Many then seek to remedy it with a "do-it-yourself" religion, which does not help us in the end, however, as experience has shown. Therefore the Pope asked the young people at World Youth Day, and all of us together with them, to help people discover Jesus Christ, the true star that shows the way. We, then, must first seek constantly to become better acquainted with him, so as to be able to guide others to him in a convincing manner. Quite important in achieving this purpose is a love for Sacred Scripture and, consequently, a knowledge of the faith of the Church "which opens up for us the meaning of Scripture", because the Holy Spirit guides the Church, "causing her to enter ever more deeply into the truth" (cf. Jn 16:13).

Pope Benedict emphasized in this regard the fundamental value of the *Catechism of the Catholic Church* and of the recent *Compendium* of it, but he added, of course, that the books by themselves are not enough: it is necessary to form communities based on the faith. In recent decades many such communities have sprung up "in which the power of the Gospel is keenly felt". Benedict XVI asked them always to strive for communion with each other and above all with the Pope and the Bishops, the guarantors of our membership in the great family of God.

Our communion in the one Body of Christ must be manifested, furthermore, in the concrete, practical details of life: in the ability to forgive and in an awareness of our need for the other person and in a willingness to share. And this leads to a commitment to our neighbor, even "those physically far away, whom we nevertheless consider to be close". Here Pope Benedict stressed the value of the various forms of volunteer work that our society so urgently needs, for example, service to the elderly and the suffering. Indeed, communion with Christ opens our eyes, leads us to discover that "it is much better to be useful and at the disposal of others than to be concerned only with the comforts that are offered to us." The Pope concluded, "I know that you as young people have great aspirations, that you want to pledge yourselves to build a better world. Let others see this, let the world see it, since this is exactly the witness that the world expects from the disciples of Jesus Christ; in this way, and through your love above all, the world will be able to discover the star that we follow as believers."

Already in his initial greeting at the Cologne-Bonn airport, Pope Benedict made clear how in World Youth Day celebrations the boundaries between continents, cultures, races and nations disappear and how we are called to be of one mind and to have one attitude of sincere and universal welcome, of dialogue and collaboration among different people, to practice "the virtue of hospitality, which has almost disappeared and is one of man's original virtues". Then, in his visit to the Synagogue, he insisted on the transcendent dignity shared by every human person, created in the image of God, and consequently on the rejection of any discrimination whatsoever among men. It was no accident, then, that the systematic attempt to exterminate the Jewish people, in the darkest period of German and European history, was the work of "an insane racist ideology, born of neo-paganism", which no longer acknowledged the sanctity of God and therefore trampled also on the sacredness of human life. With respect to relations between the Catholic Church and the Jews, Benedict XVI continued resolutely along the path set out in the conciliar Declaration *Nostra Aetate*—on which John Paul II took decisive steps—emphasizing that "we need to show respect and love for one another", also and especially in those areas in which, due to our convictions in faith, we diverge, and to direct our gaze "forward" to the tasks of today and tomorrow, making progress in the theological evaluation of the relation between the Jewish faith and Christianity and collaborating on the practical level for human rights and the sacredness of human life, family values, social justice and peace in the world. The Ten Commandments, our shared legacy and commitment, are for all of us and, in particular, for young people "not a burden, but a signpost showing the path leading to a successful life".

In his meeting with the representatives of several Muslim Communities, too, Benedict XVI cited John Paul II and the Declaration *Nostra Aetate*, which contains statements that "remain [for us] the *Magna Carta* of the dialogue with you, dear Muslim friends". In this meeting the Pope addressed very clearly and forcefully the question of terrorism, "a perverse and cruel choice which shows contempt for the sacred right to life and undermines the very foundations of all civil coexistence", and thanked the Muslim representatives for having rejected publicly any connection between their faith and terrorism. It is indeed the duty of those who are responsible for guiding and teaching, especially in dealing with the younger generations, clearly to condemn terrorism, to eliminate all feelings of rancor from their hearts, to resist all forms of intolerance and to oppose every manifestation of violence.

In reality Christians and Muslims are called to listen together to the message conveyed "by the quiet but clear voice of conscience" concerning the dignity of the human person and the defense of the rights that spring from it, which is the goal of every social endeavor and every effort to bring it to fruition. Only through recognition of the centrality of the person "can a common basis for understanding be found, one which enables us to move beyond cultural conflicts and which neutralizes the disruptive power of ideologies". The memory of the wars that were waged with both sides invoking the name of God and of the atrocities perpetrated in the name of religion ought to fill us with shame and spur us on to seek ways of reconciliation and to respect each other's identity: therefore the defense of religious freedom and respect for minorities are an ongoing imperative and a sign of true civilization.

The meeting with seminarians brings us to the heart of this relationship with Christ that Pope Benedict made the focus of the World Youth Day: he wanted to have this meeting "so that the vocational dimension would truly emerge in all of its importance", since it plays an ever more important role in such celebrations. The seminarian, indeed, "experiences the beauty of that call in a moment of grace which could be defined as 'falling in love' ", that is to say, he finds himself in an important phase of his search for a personal relationship and of his encounter with Christ, and only by having a personal experience of Christ can he understand his will and hence his own vocation: this is the task and the essential purpose of seminary education, a time set aside for formation and discernment. On the practical plane, the role of the formators is decisive for the quality of the seminary and hence of the presbyterate of a diocese. Speaking in particular to the seminarians, the Pope highlighted the figure of Mary, who enables us to see and touch Jesus, her Son, and to hold him in our arms: through his seminary experience, indeed, the seminarian no longer sees the Church "from the outside", but rather perceives her, as it were, "from the inside", as his own home, "inasmuch as she is

the home of Christ, where 'Mary his mother' dwells". Seminary training is a time of preparation for ministry [*missione*],
when each seminarian will return to live among the people as
a priest, as an *alter Christus*, and will have to confront dangers,
weariness, perplexities and doubts. In order to overcome
them, it is essential always to remember Jesus' words: "Abide in
my love" (cf. Jn 15:9). Thus we can bear much fruit, as he has
promised.

In his address to the German Bishops, Benedict XVI emphasized that this World Youth Day can be a new beginning
for pastoral work among young people in Germany, as has
been the case in the countries that have hosted previous World
Youth Day celebrations. It is a question now, above all, of
sustaining and making "definitive", so to speak, the enthusiasm
of young people, their communion in the joy of faith, which
only the Lord can create. The Pope admitted that there are
"wrinkles" on the face of the Church in Germany as well and
many challenges that she must confront, often including the
need for "a true and proper first evangelization", as some of
the German Bishops have already stressed. Furthermore he
offered clear guidelines on the priority that should be given to
adoring God and Jesus Christ, on catechesis, on the pastoral
care of vocations, on the pastoral care of families, on lay associations and movements and their relationship with the local
Church and the parish. But he likewise accented the vitality
and positive energies of this Church [in Germany], which
wants to be open to the future, which is young and ever new
because the source of the Church's youthfulness is the eternity
of God, the visibility of Christ through her, which is not, on
the contrary, "a matter of pandering to youth, which is basically ridiculous". The practical union of the Bishops among
themselves and with the Successor of Peter, which springs
from the Eucharist, was the final note in the affectionate message of Benedict XVI to the German Bishops.

The ecumenical meeting, more than any other, gave the
Pope the opportunity to confirm, following the teachings of

the [Second Vatican] Council, Paul VI and John Paul II, that the recovery of full and visible unity among Christians is a priority of his Pontificate. Consequently ecumenical dialogue is indispensable: it takes on particular importance in Germany, the country in which the Reformation began, yet also one of the countries in which the twentieth-century ecumenical movement got under way. Over the years the dialogue has helped us to rediscover our real Christian brotherhood, a fraternity that "is not just a vague sentiment [or] . . . a sign of indifference to truth" but that is founded on the supernatural reality of the one Baptism, which makes us all members of the one Body of Christ. As one fruit of this dialogue, Benedict XVI recalled in particular the *Joint Declaration on the Doctrine of Justification* (1999), and he added that he, too, like many Christians in Germany, expects "further concrete steps to bring us closer together". In this regard, prior to the ecclesiological questions and to those concerning ministry, it is the "personal opinion" of Pope Benedict that the real question is "the presence of the Word in the world": specifically, the interrelatedness of the Word of God, the witnesses to this Word in the Apostolic Succession and the *regula fidei* [rule of faith] as the key to interpreting it. An urgent priority in the ecumenical dialogue, then, are the great ethical questions of today; in this area we are called to give, even more than in the past, a common witness that is unambiguous, so as not to fall short of our duty as believers in Christ in addressing the people of our time.

In addressing the basic question about the purpose of ecumenism, "what does it mean to reestablish unity among all Christians?", the Pope clearly stated that, according to Catholics, the full visible unity of the disciples of Jesus Christ subsists in the Catholic Church, without the possibility of ever being lost: this unity, however, does not mean an "ecumenism of return", that is, it does not require other Christians to deny their own faith history, and it does not imply uniformity in all expressions of theology and spirituality or in liturgical forms or matters of discipline. We cannot "bring about" this unity by our own powers; rather, it can only be the gift of the Holy Spirit. Consequently, spiritual ecumenism, that is, prayer, conversion and the sanctification of life, constitutes the heart of the encounter and of the ecumenical movement. Therefore the current development of a "network" of spiritual links among Catholics and Christians from the various Churches and Ecclesial Communities is an encouraging reason for optimism.

In his twelve talks at the Twentieth World Youth Day, Pope Benedict naturally had quite a few occasions to manifest his own joy over returning, as the Successor of Peter, to his own land and to demonstrate his love for Germany by recalling the memories and ties that unite him to Cologne. Especially in his address to the young people on *Roncalliplatz* [Roncalli Square], after visiting the Cathedral of Cologne, he left some room for pertinent autobiographical notes. The atmosphere of joy, confidence and friendship also prompted him, in some circumstances, to improvise witty remarks that are a delight to read. From the collection of texts emerges, above all, together with the joy, a sense of heartfelt gratitude to God, accompanied by sincere appreciation for those who in any way contributed to making possible this first World Youth Day of Pope Benedict.

Reading this little book will reinforce our conviction that the Lord has given us, in the person of the new Pontiff, a great Teacher of the faith and at the same time a Pastor who knows the way that can lead us to intimacy with God: a catechist of extraordinary depth and clarity who is, however, even before that, an evangelizer who knows how to compel his listeners gently to pay attention to Christ. From him will come a further impetus and direction for the pastoral care of young people and for the pastoral ministry in general.

A particular charism of his, which emerged even more forcefully in Cologne, is an ability to combine universal openness with Catholic identity, clear and comprehensive witness to the truth of Christ with the gentleness of fraternal charity, according to the words of the First Letter of Peter (3:15): "In your hearts reverence Christ as Lord. Always be prepared to make a defense to any one who calls you to account for the hope that is in you, yet do it with gentleness and reverence."

With Benedict XVI, therefore, we are seeing a continuation of that happy decree of Providence, which was made particularly manifest in John Paul II and in the other Popes of the last century, whereby an opening to the mystery of God becomes somehow tangible at the institutional summit of the Church. It is less difficult, therefore, to understand that the human and earthly dimension of the Church is not separate from the theological and supernatural dimension and that, in the final analysis, salvation is not something that is far away from us.

In his interview on Vatican Radio before his journey to Cologne, the new Pope expressly remarked that he personally would never have dared to choose Germany as the destination of his first trip abroad. "But if it is the good God himself who makes these arrangements, we surely have the right to enjoy them!" Not only his compatriots but all of us as well share in this joy and cherish the hope that Benedict XVI will be a great blessing, particularly for believers in Germany.

In the same spirit we pray that the fruits of the Twentieth World Youth Day will be lasting and that its legacy will be lively and dynamic, in the day-to-day pastoral ministry of our Churches as well as in the consciences and the lives of the young people, until they meet again in Sydney, Australia, in 2008 and beyond, with the Lord who is coming.

CAMILLO CARDINAL RUINI

Vicar-General of the Pope for the Diocese of Rome

MESSAGE OF THE HOLY FATHER
JOHN PAUL II
TO THE YOUTH OF THE WORLD
ON THE OCCASION OF
THE TWENTIETH WORLD YOUTH DAY
(COLOGNE, AUGUST 2005)

CASTEL GANDOLFO / 6 AUGUST 2004

"We have come to worship him" (Mt 2:2)

My Dear Young People!

1. This year we have celebrated the *Nineteenth World Youth Day*, meditating on the desire expressed by some Greeks who had gone to Jerusalem for the Passover: *"We wish to see Jesus"* (Jn 12:21). And here we are now, making our way to Cologne where, in August 2005, the *Twentieth World Youth Day* is to be celebrated.

"We have come to worship him" (Mt 2:2): this is the theme of the next World Youth Day. It is a theme that enables young people from every continent to follow in spirit the path taken by the Magi, whose relics, according to a pious tradition, are venerated in this very city, and to meet, as they did, the Messiah of all nations.

It is true to say that the light of Christ had already opened the minds and the hearts of the Magi. "They went their way" (Mt 2:9), says the Evangelist, setting out boldly along unknown paths on a long, and by no means easy, journey. They did not hesitate to leave everything behind in order to follow the star that they had seen in the East (cf. Mt 2:2). Imitating the Magi, you young people are also making preparations to set out on a "journey" from every region of the world to go to Cologne. It is important for you not only to concern yourselves with the practical arrangements for World Youth Day, but first of all you must carefully prepare yourselves spiritually, in an atmosphere of faith and listening to the Word of God.

2. *"And the star . . . went before them, till it came to rest over the place where the child was"* (Mt 2:9). The Magi reached Bethlehem because they had obediently allowed themselves to be guided by the star. Indeed, *"When they saw the star, they rejoiced exceedingly with great joy"* (Mt 2:10). It is important, my dear friends, to learn to *observe the signs* with which God is calling us and guiding us. When we are conscious of being led by him, our heart experiences *authentic and deep joy* as well as a powerful desire to meet him and a persevering strength to follow him obediently.

"And going into the house they saw the child with Mary his mother" (Mt 2:11). There is nothing extraordinary about this at first sight. Yet that Child was different from any other: he is the only Son of God, yet he *emptied himself of his glory* (cf. Phil 2:7) and came to earth to die on the Cross. He came down among us and became poor in order to reveal to us his divine glory, which we shall contemplate fully in heaven, our blessed home.

Who could have invented a greater sign of love? We are left in awe before *the mystery of a God who lowered himself* to take on our human condition, to the point of giving his life for us on the Cross (cf. Phil 2:6–8). In his *poverty*—as Saint Paul reminds us—*"though he was rich, yet for your sake he became poor, so that by his poverty you might become rich"* (2 Cor 8:9), and came to offer salvation to sinners. How can we give thanks to God for such magnanimous goodness?

3. The Magi found Jesus at *"Bêth-lehem"*, which means *"house of bread"*. In the humble stable in Bethlehem on some straw lay the *"grain of wheat"* who, by dying, would bring forth *"much fruit"* (cf. Jn 12:24). When speaking of himself and his saving mission in the course of his public life, Jesus would later use the image of bread. He would say, *"I am the bread of life"*, *"I am the bread which came down from heaven"*, *"the bread that I shall give for the life of the world is my flesh"* (Jn 6:35, 41, 51).

Faithfully pursuing the path of our Redeemer from the poverty of the *Crib* to his abandonment on the *Cross*, we can better understand the mystery of his love which redeems humanity. The Child, laid by Mary in the manger, is the Man-God we shall see nailed to the Cross. The same Redeemer is present in the Sacrament of the Eucharist. In the *stable at Bethlehem* he allowed himself to be worshipped under the humble outward appearances of a newborn baby, by Mary, by Joseph and by the shepherds; in the *consecrated Host* we adore him sacramentally present in his Body, Blood, soul and Godhead, and he offers himself to us as the food of eternal life. The *Mass* then becomes a truly loving encounter with the One who gave himself wholly for us. Do not hesitate, my dear young friends, to respond to him when he invites you *"to the wedding feast of the Lamb"* (cf. Rev 19:9). Listen to him, prepare yourselves properly and draw close to the Sacrament of the Altar, particularly in this Year of the Eucharist (October 2004–2005) which I have proclaimed for the whole Church.

4. *"They fell down and worshipped him"* (Mt 2:11). While the Magi acknowledged and worshipped the baby that Mary cradled in her arms as the One awaited by the nations and foretold by prophets, today we can also worship him in the Eucharist and *acknowledge him as our Creator, our only Lord and Savior.*

"Opening their treasures they offered him gifts, gold and frankincense and myrrh" (Mt 2:11). The gifts that the Magi offered the Messiah symbolized true worship. With gold, they emphasized his Royal Godhead; with incense, they acknowledged him as the priest of the New Covenant; by offering him myrrh, they celebrated the prophet who would shed his own blood to reconcile humanity with the Father.

My dear young people, you too offer to the Lord the gold of your lives, namely, *your freedom* to follow him out of love, responding faithfully to his call; let the incense of your fervent *prayer* rise up to him, in praise of his glory; offer him your myrrh, *that is your affection of total gratitude to him*, true Man, who loved us to the point of dying as a criminal on Golgotha.

5. Be worshippers of the only true God, giving him pride

of place in your lives! *Idolatry* is an ever-present temptation. Sadly, there are those who seek the solution to their problems *in religious practices that are incompatible with the Christian faith.* There is a strong urge to believe in the facile myths of success and power; it is dangerous to accept the fleeting ideas of the sacred which present God in the form of cosmic energy, or in any other manner that is inconsistent with Catholic teaching.

My dear young people, do not yield to *false illusions* and *passing fads* which so frequently leave behind a tragic spiritual vacuum! Reject the *seduction* of wealth, consumerism and the subtle violence sometimes used by the mass media.

Worshipping the true God is an authentic act of *resistance to all forms of idolatry.* Worship Christ: He is the Rock on which to build your future and a world of greater justice and solidarity. Jesus is *the Prince of peace*: the source of forgiveness and reconciliation, who can make brothers and sisters of all the members of the human family.

6. *"And they departed to their own country by another way"* (Mt 2:12). The Gospel tells us that after their meeting with Christ, the Magi returned home "by another way". This change of route can symbolize the *conversion* to which all those who encounter Jesus are called, in order to become the true worshippers that he desires (cf. Jn 4:23–24). This entails imitating the way he acted by becoming, as the apostle Paul writes, *"a living sacrifice, holy and acceptable to God"*. The apostle then adds that we must not be conformed to the mentality of this world, but be transformed by the renewal of our minds, to *"prove what is the will of God, what is good and acceptable and perfect"* (cf. Rom 12:1–2).

Listening to Christ and worshipping him leads us to make *courageous choices*, to take what are sometimes heroic decisions. Jesus is demanding, because he wishes our genuine happiness. He calls some to give up everything to follow him in the priestly or consecrated life. Those who hear this invitation must not be afraid to say "yes" and generously to set about following him as his disciples. But in addition to vocations to special forms of consecration there is also the specific vocation of all baptized Christians: that is also a vocation to that "high standard" of ordinary Christian living which is expressed in holiness (cf. *Novo Millennio Ineunte*, no. 31). When we meet Christ and accept his Gospel, life changes and we are driven to communicate our experience to others.

There are so many of our contemporaries who do not yet know the love of God or who are seeking to fill their hearts with trifling substitutes. It is therefore urgently necessary for us to be *witnesses to love contemplated in Christ*. The invitation to take part in *World Youth Day* is also extended to you, dear friends, who are not baptized or who do not identify with the Church. Are you not perhaps yearning for the Absolute and in search of "something" to give a meaning to your lives? Turn to Christ, and you will not be let down.

7. Dear young people, the Church needs genuine witnesses for the new evangelization: men and women whose lives have been transformed by meeting with Jesus, men and women who are capable of communicating this experience to others. The Church needs saints. All are called to holiness, and holy people alone can renew humanity. Many have gone before us along this path of Gospel heroism, and I urge you to turn often to them to pray for their intercession. By meeting in Cologne you will learn to become better acquainted with some of them, such as *Saint Boniface*, the apostle of Germany; the *Saints of Cologne*; and in particular Ursula, Albert the Great, Teresa Benedicta of the Cross (Edith Stein) and Blessed Adolph Kolping. Of these I would like to mention specifically *Saint Albert and Teresa Benedicta of the Cross*, who, with the same interior attitude as the Magi, were passionate seekers after the truth. They had no hesitation in placing their intellectual abilities at the service of the faith, thereby demonstrating that faith and reason are linked and seek each other.

My dear young people as you move forward in spirit towards Cologne, the Pope will accompany you with his prayers. May Mary, "Eucharistic woman" and Mother of Wisdom, support you along the way, enlighten your decisions, and teach you to love what is true, good and beautiful. May she lead you all to her Son, who alone can satisfy the innermost yearnings of the human mind and heart.

Go with my blessing!

JOHN PAUL II

APOSTOLIC JOURNEY TO COLOGNE
ON THE OCCASION OF
THE TWENTIETH WORLD YOUTH DAY

WELCOME CEREMONY

ADDRESS OF HIS HOLINESS POPE BENEDICT XVI

COLOGNE AIRPORT / THURSDAY, 18 AUGUST 2005

Mr. President of the Republic,
Distinguished Political and Civil Authorities,
Your Eminences and Venerable Brothers in the Episcopate,
Dear Citizens of the Federal Republic,
My Dear Young People,

Today, with deep joy I find myself for the first time after my election to the Chair of Peter in my beloved Homeland, in Germany. I can only repeat what I stated at an interview with Vatican Radio. I consider it a loving gesture of reconciliation since, quite unintentionally, my first Visit outside of Italy should be to my Homeland: Here in Cologne, at a moment, in a place and on an occasion when the young people of all the world are meeting, from all the continents, in which the frontiers between the continents, cultures, races, nations disappear, in order that we may all be one thanks to the star that has shone for us: the star of faith in Jesus Christ, which unites us and shows us the way so that we can all be a great force for peace beyond all frontiers and all divisions.

I thank God for this with deep emotion, that he has enabled me to begin here in my Country and on such a propitious occasion for peace.

Therefore, as you have said, Mr. President, I have come to Cologne in very deep continuity with my great and beloved Predecessor John Paul II, who had this intuition—I should say this inspiration—of the World Youth Days, in this way creating an occasion not only of exceptional religious and ecclesial meaning, but also human, which takes people beyond the borderlines between one and the other and contributes to building a common future.

I am sincerely grateful to all present for the warm welcome given to me. My respectful greeting goes first to the President of the Federal Republic, Mr. Horst Köhler, whom I thank for the gracious words of welcome which he warmly addressed to me. I did not know an economist could also be a philosopher and a theologian! My heartfelt thanks.

I also express my respect and gratitude to the Representatives of the Government, the Members of the Diplomatic Corps and the civil and military Authorities, the Federal Chancellor, the President of Nordrhein-Westfalen, all the Authorities present here.

With fraternal affection I greet the Pastor of the Archdiocese of Cologne, Cardinal Joachim Meisner. My greeting also goes to the other Bishops, with the President of the German Bishops' Conference, Cardinal Lehmann, the priests, men and women Religious, and to all those engaged in various pastoral activities in the German-speaking Dioceses.

At this moment I also wish to greet with affection all those living in the different *Länder* of the Federal Republic of Germany.

In these days of intense preparation for World Youth Day, the Dioceses of Germany, and the Diocese and City of Cologne in particular, have been enlivened by the presence of very many young people from different parts of the world. I thank all those who have so competently and generously helped to organize this worldwide ecclesial event.

I am grateful to the parishes, religious institutes, associations, civil organizations and private citizens who have thoughtfully offered hospitality and so friendly a welcome to the thousands of pilgrims coming here from different continents. It is a fine thing that on such occasions the virtue of hospitality, which has almost disappeared and is one of man's original virtues, should be renewed and enable people of all states of life to meet.

The Church in Germany and the People of the German Federal Republic can be proud of their long tradition of openness to the global community; among other things, this is seen in their many initiatives of solidarity, particularly on behalf of developing countries.

In this spirit of esteem and acceptance towards all those who come from different cultures and traditions, we are about to experience *World Youth Day in Cologne*. That so many young people have come to meet the Successor of Peter is a sign of the Church's vitality. I am happy to be with them, to confirm their faith and, God willing, to enliven their hope.

At the same time, I am sure that I will also receive something from the young people, that their enthusiasm, their sensitivity and their readiness will sustain me and give me the courage to continue my journey in the service of the Church as the Successor of Peter and to face the challenges of the future.

To all of you present here, and all those who have welcomed people from other parts of the world in these event-filled days, I now express my most cordial greeting.

In addition to intense moments of prayer, reflection and celebration with them and with all those taking part in the various scheduled events, I will have an opportunity to meet the Bishops, to whom even now I extend my fraternal greeting. I will also meet the representatives of the other Churches and Ecclesial Communities. I shall be honored to make a Visit to the Synagogue, which I have very much at heart, for a meeting with the Jewish community, and also to welcome the representatives of some Islamic communities.

These meetings are important steps to intensify the journey of dialogue and cooperation in our shared commitment to building a more just and fraternal future, a future which is truly more human. We all know how necessary it is to seek this path, how much we need this dialogue and this cooperation.

During this *World Youth Day* we will reflect together on the theme: "*We have come to worship him*" (Mt 2:2). This is a precious opportunity for thinking more deeply about the meaning of human life as a "pilgrimage", a journey guided by a "star", in search of the Lord.

Together we shall consider the Magi, who would never have thought to become pilgrims even after death, nor that one day their relics would be carried in pilgrimage to Cologne. We shall look to these personages who, coming from different lands, were among the first to recognize the promised Messiah in Jesus of Nazareth, the Son of the Virgin Mary, and to bow down in worship before him (cf. Mt 2:1–12).

The Ecclesial Community and the city of Cologne have a special link with these emblematic figures. Like the Magi, all believers—and young people in particular—have been called to set out on the journey of life in search of truth, justice and love. We must seek this star, we must follow it. The ultimate goal of the journey can be found only through an encounter with Christ, an encounter which cannot take place without faith.

Along this interior journey we can be guided by the many signs with which a long and rich Christian tradition has indelibly marked this Land of Germany: from great historical monuments to countless works of art found throughout the Country, from documents preserved in libraries to lively popular traditions, from philosophical inquiry to the theological reflection of her many great thinkers, from the spiritual traditions to the mystical experience of a vast array of saints.

Here we find a very rich cultural and spiritual heritage which even today, in the heart of Europe, testifies to the fruitfulness of the Christian faith and tradition which we must rekindle, because it has within it new strength for the future.

The Diocese and the region of Cologne, in particular, keep the living memory of great witnesses who, as it were, are present in the pilgrimage begun by the three Magi. I think of Saint Boniface, Saint Ursula, Saint Albert the Great, and, in more recent times, Saint Teresa Benedicta of the Cross (Edith Stein) and Blessed Adolph Kolping.

These, our illustrious brothers and sisters in the faith, who down the centuries have held high the torch of holiness, have become people who have seen the star and have shown it to others. May these figures be "models" and "patrons" of this meeting of ours, of the World Youth Day.

While to all of you here present I renew my deep gratitude for your gracious welcome, I pray to the Lord for the future of the Church and of society as a whole in this Federal Republic of Germany, so dear to me. May this Country's long history and her great social, economic and cultural attainments be an incentive to renewed commitment on your journey at a time when new problems and issues are also facing the other peoples of the Continent.

May the Virgin Mary, who presented the Child Jesus to the Magi when they arrived in Bethlehem to worship the Savior, continue to intercede for us, just as for centuries she has kept watch over the German People from her many shrines throughout the German *Länder*.

May the Lord bless everyone here present, together with all the pilgrims and all who live in this Land.

May God protect the Federal Republic of Germany!

To the Young People

CELEBRATION WELCOMING
THE YOUNG PEOPLE

ADDRESS OF HIS HOLINESS POPE BENEDICT XVI

COLOGNE—POLLER RHEINWIESEN / THURSDAY, 18 AUGUST 2005

Dear Young People,

I am delighted to meet you here in Cologne on the banks of the Rhine! You have come from various parts of Germany, Europe and the rest of the world as pilgrims in the footsteps of the Magi.

Following their route, you too want to find Jesus. Like them, you have begun this journey in order to contemplate, both personally and with others, the face of God revealed by the Child in the manger.

Like yourselves, I too have set out to join you in kneeling before the consecrated white Host in which the eyes of faith recognize the Real Presence of the Savior of the world. Together, we will continue to meditate on the theme of this *World Youth Day*: "*We have come to worship him*" (Mt 2:2).

With great joy I welcome you, dear young people. You have come here from near and far, walking the streets of the world and the pathways of life. My particular greeting goes to those who, like the Magi, have come from the East. You are the representatives of so many of our brothers and sisters who are waiting, without realizing it, for the star to rise in their skies and lead them to Christ, Light of the Nations, in whom they will find the fullest response to their hearts' deepest desires.

I also greet with affection those among you who have not been baptized and those of you who do not yet know Christ or have not yet found a home in his Church. Pope John Paul II had invited you in particular to come to this gathering; I thank you for deciding to come to Cologne.

Some of you might perhaps describe your adolescence in the words with which Edith Stein, who later lived in the Carmel in Cologne, described her own: "I consciously and deliberately lost the habit of praying." During these days, you can once again have a moving experience of prayer as dialogue with God, the God who we know loves us and whom we in turn wish to love.

To all of you I appeal: Open wide your hearts to God! Let yourselves be surprised by Christ! Let him have "the right of free speech" during these days!

Open the doors of your freedom to his merciful love! Share your joys and pains with Christ, and let him enlighten your minds with his light and touch your hearts with his grace.

In these days blessed with sharing and joy, may you have a liberating experience of the Church as the place where God's merciful love reaches out to all people. In the Church and through the Church you will meet Christ, who is waiting for you.

Today, as I arrive in Cologne to take part with you in the *Twentieth World Youth Day*, I naturally recall with deep gratitude the Servant of God so greatly loved by us all, Pope John Paul II, who had the inspired idea of calling young people from all over the world to join in celebrating Christ, the one Redeemer of the human race. Thanks to the profound dialogue which developed over more than twenty years between the Pope and young people, many of them were able to deepen their faith, forge bonds of communion, develop a love for the Good News of salvation in Christ and a desire to proclaim it throughout the world.

That great Pope understood the challenges faced by young people today, and, as a sign of his trust in them, he did not hesitate to spur them on to be courageous heralds of the Gospel and intrepid builders of the civilization of truth, love and peace.

Today, it is my turn to take up this extraordinary spiritual legacy bequeathed to us by Pope John Paul II. He loved you— you realized that, and you returned his love with all your youthful enthusiasm. Now all of us together have to put his teaching into practice. It is this commitment which has brought us here to Cologne, as pilgrims in the footsteps of the Magi.

According to tradition, the names of the Magi in Greek were Melchior, Gaspar and Balthasar. Matthew, in his Gospel, tells of the question which burned in the hearts of the Magi: "Where is the infant king of the Jews?" (Mt 2:2). It was in order to search for him that they set out on the long journey to Jerusalem. This was why they withstood hardships and sacrifices and never yielded to discouragement or the temptation to give up and go home. Now that they were close to their goal, they had no other question than this.

We too have come to Cologne because in our hearts we have the same urgent question that prompted the Magi from the East to set out on their journey, even if it is differently expressed.

It is true that today we are no longer looking for a king, but we are concerned for the state of the world and we are asking: "Where do I find standards to live by, what are the criteria that govern responsible cooperation in building the present and the future of our world? On whom can I rely? To whom shall I entrust myself? Where is the One who can offer me the response capable of satisfying my heart's deepest desires?"

The fact that we ask questions like these means that we realize our journey is not over until we meet the One who has the power to establish that universal Kingdom of justice and peace to which all people aspire, but which they are unable to build by themselves. Asking such questions also means searching for Someone who can neither deceive nor be deceived, and who therefore can offer a certainty so solid that we can live for it and, if need be, even die for it.

Dear friends, when questions like these appear on the horizon of life, we must be able to make the necessary choices. It is like finding ourselves at a crossroads: Which direction do we take? The one prompted by the passions or the one indicated by the star which shines in your conscience?

The Magi heard the answer: "In Bethlehem of Judea; for so it is written by the prophet" (Mt 2:5), and, enlightened by these words, they chose to press forward to the very end. From Jerusalem they went on to Bethlehem. In other words, they went from the word which showed them where to find the King of the Jews whom they were seeking, all the way to the end, to an encounter with the King who was at the same time the Lamb of God who takes away the sins of the world.

Those words are also spoken for us. We too have a choice to make. If we think about it, this is precisely our experience when we share in the Eucharist. For in every Mass the encounter with the Word of God introduces us to our participation in the mystery of the Cross and Resurrection of Christ and, hence, introduces us to the Eucharistic Meal, to union with Christ. Present on the altar is the One whom the Magi saw lying in the manger: Christ, the living Bread who came down from heaven to give life to the world, the true Lamb who gives his own life for the salvation of mankind.

Enlightened by the Word, it is in Bethlehem—the "House of Bread"—that we can always encounter the inconceivable greatness of a God who humbled himself even to appearing in a manger, to giving himself as food on the altar.

We can imagine the awe which the Magi experienced before the Child in swaddling clothes. Only faith enabled them to recognize in the face of that Child the King whom they were seeking, the God to whom the star had guided them. In him, crossing the abyss between the finite and the infinite, the visible and the invisible, the Eternal entered time, the Mystery became known by entrusting himself to us in the frail body of a small child.

"The Magi are filled with awe by what they see; heaven on

earth and earth in heaven; man in God and God in man; they see enclosed in a tiny body the One whom the entire world cannot contain" (*Saint Peter Chrysologus*, Serm. 160, no. 2).

In these days, during this "Year of the Eucharist", we will turn with the same awe to Christ present in the Tabernacle of Mercy, in the Sacrament of the Altar.

Dear young people, the happiness you are seeking, the happiness you have a right to enjoy has a name and a face: it is Jesus of Nazareth, hidden in the Eucharist. Only he gives the fullness of life to humanity! With Mary, say your own "yes" to God, for he wishes to give himself to you.

I repeat today what I said at the beginning of my Pontificate: "If we let Christ into our lives, we lose nothing, nothing, absolutely nothing of what makes life free, beautiful and great. No! Only in this friendship are the doors of life opened wide. Only in this friendship is the great potential of human existence truly revealed. Only in this friendship do we experience beauty and liberation" (*Homily at the Mass of Inauguration*, 24 April 2005).

Be completely convinced of this: Christ takes from you nothing that is beautiful and great, but brings everything to perfection for the glory of God, the happiness of men and women, and the salvation of the world.

In these days I encourage you to commit yourselves without reserve to serving Christ, whatever the cost. The encounter with Jesus Christ will allow you to experience in your hearts the joy of his living and life-giving presence and enable you to bear witness to it before others. Let your presence in this city be the first sign and proclamation of the Gospel, thanks to the witness of your actions and your joy.

Let us raise our hearts in a hymn of praise and thanksgiving to the Father for the many blessings he has given us and for the gift of faith which we will celebrate together, making it manifest to the world from this land in the heart of Europe, a Europe which owes so much to the Gospel and its witnesses down the centuries.

And now I shall go as a pilgrim to the Cathedral of Cologne, to venerate the relics of the holy Magi who left everything to follow the star which was guiding them to the Savior of the human race. You too, dear young people, have already had, or will have, the opportunity to make the same pilgrimage.

These relics are only the poor and frail sign of what those men were and what they experienced so many centuries ago. The relics direct us towards God himself: it is he who, by the power of his grace, grants to weak human beings the courage to bear witness to him before the world.

By inviting us to venerate the mortal remains of the martyrs and saints, the Church does not forget that, in the end, these are indeed just human bones, but they are bones that belonged to individuals touched by the living power of God. The relics of the saints are traces of that invisible but real presence which sheds light upon the shadows of the world and reveals the Kingdom of Heaven in our midst. They cry out with us and for us: "Maranatha!"—"Come, Lord Jesus!"

My dear friends, I make these words my farewell, and I invite you to the Saturday evening Vigil. I shall see you then!

VISIT TO THE CATHEDRAL OF COLOGNE

ADDRESS OF HIS HOLINESS POPE BENEDICT XVI

COLOGNE—RONCALLIPLATZ / THURSDAY, 18 AUGUST 2005

Dear Brothers and Sisters,

I am pleased to be with you this evening, in this city of Cologne to which I am bound by so many beautiful memories. I spent the first years of my academic career in Bonn, unforgettable years of the reawakening of youth, of hope before the Council, years in which I often came to Cologne and learned to love this Rome of the North.

Here one breathes the great history, and the flow of the river brings openness to the world. It is a meeting place, a place of culture. I have always loved the spirit, sense of humor, joyfulness and intelligence of its inhabitants. Besides, I have to say, I loved the catholicity that Cologne's inhabitants have in their blood, for Christians have existed here for almost 2,000 years, so that this catholicity has penetrated the character of the inhabitants in the sense of a joyful religiosity.

Let us rejoice in this today. Cologne can give young people something of its joyful catholicity, which is at the same time both old and young.

It was very beautiful for me that Cardinal Frings gave me his full confidence from the very first, making an authentically fatherly friendship with me. Then, despite my youth and lack of experience, he gave me the great gift of summoning me as his theologian, of bringing me to Rome so that I could take part beside him in the Second Vatican Council and live this extraordinary historical event from close at hand, making some small contribution to it.

I also became acquainted with Cardinal Höffner, then Bishop of Münster, to whom I was likewise bound by a deep and lively friendship. Thanks be to God that this chain of friendships was never broken. Cardinal Meisner has also been my friend for a very long time, so that beginning with Frings and continuing with Höffner and Meisner, I have always been able to feel at home here in Cologne.

I think the time has now come to say "thank you" to so many people with the strong, deep voice of the heart.

In the first place, let us thank the good Lord who gives us the beautiful blue sky and his tangible blessing these days. Let us thank the Mother of God, who has taken the direction of World Youth Day into her hands.

I thank Cardinal Meisner and all his collaborators; Cardinal Lehmann, President of the German Bishops' Conference, and with him, all the Bishops of the German Dioceses, in particular the planning committee in Cologne, but also the Dioceses and local communities which have welcomed the young people in recent days. I can well imagine what all of this entails in terms of energy spent and sacrifices accepted, and I pray that it will bear abundant fruit in the spiritual success of this *World Youth Day*.

Finally, I cannot fail to express my profound gratitude to the civil and military Authorities, the leaders of the city and region, and the police and security forces of Germany and North Rhine-Westphalia. In the person of the Mayor I thank the people of Cologne for their understanding in the face of this "invasion" by so many young people from all over the world.

The city of Cologne would not be what it is without the Magi, who have had so great an impact on its history, its culture and its faith. Here, in some sense, the Church celebrates the Feast of the Epiphany every day of the year! And so, before addressing you, dear inhabitants of Cologne, before greeting you, I wanted to pause for a few moments of prayer before the reliquary of the three Magi, giving thanks to God for their witness of faith, hope and love.

You should know that in 1164 the relics of the Magi were escorted by the Archbishop of Cologne, Reinald von Dassel, from Milan, across the Alps, all the way to Cologne, where they were received with great jubilation. On their pilgrimage across Europe these relics left visible traces behind them which still live on today, both in place names and in popular devotions.

In honor of the Magi the inhabitants of Cologne produced the most exquisite reliquary of the whole Christian world and raised above it an even greater reliquary: Cologne Cathedral. Along with Jerusalem the "Holy City", Rome the "Eternal City" and Santiago de Compostela in Spain, Cologne, thanks to the Magi, has become down the centuries one of the most important places of pilgrimage in the Christian West.

I do not want here to continue to sing the praises of Cologne, although it would be possible and meaningful to do so; it would take too long, for it would be necessary to say too many important and beautiful things about Cologne.

However, I would like to recall that we venerate Saint Ursula and her companions here; that in 745 the Holy Father named Saint Boniface Archbishop of Cologne; that Saint Albert the Great, one of the most learned scholars of the Middle Ages, worked here and that his relics are venerated in the Church of Saint Andrew; that Thomas Aquinas, the greatest theologian of the West, studied and taught here; that in the nineteenth century Adolph Kolping founded an important social institution; that Edith Stein, a converted Jew, lived here in Cologne at the Carmelite Convent before being forced to flee to the Convent of Echt in Holland to be deported subsequently to Auschwitz, where she died a martyr. Thanks to these and all the other figures, both known and unknown, Cologne possesses a rich legacy of saints.

I would like to add that, at least as far as I know, here in Cologne one of the Magi has been identified as a Moorish King of Africa, so that a representative of the African Continent has been seen as one of Jesus Christ's first witnesses.

I would also like to add that it was here in Cologne that important exemplary initiatives sprang up whose action has spread across the world, namely: *Misereor, Adveniat* and *Renovabis.*

Now you yourselves are here, dear young people from throughout the world. You represent those distant peoples who came to know Christ through the Magi and who were brought together as the new People of God, the Church, which gathers men and women from every culture.

Today, it is your task, dear young people, to live and breathe the Church's universality. Let yourselves be inflamed by the fire of the Spirit, so that a new Pentecost may be created among you and renew the Church.

Through you, may other young people everywhere come to recognize in Christ the true answer to their deepest aspirations, and may they open their hearts to receive the Word of God Incarnate, who died and rose so that God might dwell among us and give us the truth, love and joy for which we are all yearning.

God bless these days!

MEETING WITH SEMINARIANS

ADDRESS OF HIS HOLINESS POPE BENEDICT XVI

COLOGNE—SAINT PANTALEON / FRIDAY, 19 AUGUST 2005

Dear Brothers in the Episcopate and in the Priesthood,
Dear Seminarians,

I greet all of you with great affection and gratitude for your festive welcome and particularly for the fact that you have come to this gathering from so many countries the world over. Here we are truly a spectacular image of the Catholic Church in the world.

I thank especially the seminarian, the priest and the Bishop who have given us their own personal witness. I must say that I was moved to see these paths on which the Lord has guided these men in an unexpected way and not according to their own projects.

I cordially thank you and am very pleased to have this meeting. I had asked—and this has already been said—that the *program of these days in Cologne* should include a special meeting with young seminarians, so that the vocational dimension would truly emerge in all of its importance, since it plays an ever more important role in the *World Youth Days*. It seems to me that the rain too that is falling from heaven is a blessing.

You are seminarians, that is to say, young people devoting an intense period of your lives to seeking a personal relationship with Christ, an encounter with him, in preparation for your important mission in the Church. This is what a seminary is: more than a place, it is a significant time in the life of a follower of Jesus.

I can imagine the echo that resounds in your hearts from the words of the theme of this *Twentieth World Youth Day*—"*We have come to worship him*"—and the entire moving narration of the searching and finding of the Wise Men. Each in his own way—we consider the three witnesses we have just heard—is like them: he sees a star, sets out on his journey, must, too, face what is unclear and is able to arrive at his destination under God's guidance.

This evangelical passage of the Wise Men who search out and find Jesus has a special meaning precisely for you, dear seminarians, because you are on an authentic journey, engaged in discerning—and this is a true journey—and confirming your call to the priesthood. Let us pause and reflect on this theme.

Why did the Magi set off from afar to go to Bethlehem? The answer has to do with the mystery of the "star" which they saw "in the East" and which they recognized as the star of the "King of the Jews", that is to say, the sign of the birth of the Messiah (cf. Mt 2:2). So their journey was inspired by a powerful hope, strengthened and guided by the star, which led them towards the King of the Jews, towards the kingship of God himself. This is the meaning behind our journey: to serve the kingship of God in the world.

The Magi set out because of a deep desire which prompted them to leave everything and begin a journey. It was as though they had always been waiting for that star. It was as if the journey had always been a part of their destiny and was finally about to begin.

Dear friends, this is the mystery of God's call, the mystery of vocation. It is part of the life of every Christian, but it is particularly evident in those whom Christ asks to leave every-thing in order to follow him more closely.

The seminarian experiences the beauty of that call in a moment of grace which could be defined as "falling in love". His soul is filled with amazement, which makes him ask in prayer: "Lord, why me?" But love knows no "why"; it is a free gift to which one responds with the gift of self.

The seminary years are devoted to formation and discernment. Formation, as you well know, has different strands which converge in the unity of the person: it includes human, spiritual and cultural dimensions. Its deepest goal is to bring the student to an intimate knowledge of the God who has revealed his face in Jesus Christ.

For this, in-depth study of Sacred Scripture is needed, and also of the faith and life of the Church in which the Scripture dwells as the Word of life. This must all be linked with the questions prompted by our reason and with the broader context of modern life.

Such study can at times seem arduous, but it is an indispensable part of our encounter with Christ and our vocation to proclaim him. All this is aimed at shaping a steady and balanced personality, one capable of receiving validly and fulfilling responsibly the priestly mission.

The role of formators is decisive: the quality of the presbyterate in a particular Church depends greatly on that of the seminary, and consequently on the quality of those responsible for formation.

Dear seminarians, for this very reason we pray today with genuine gratitude for your superiors, professors and educators, who are spiritually present at this meeting. Let us ask the Lord to help them carry out as well as possible the important task entrusted to them.

The seminary years are a time of journeying, of exploration, but above all of discovering Christ. It is only when a young man has had a personal experience of Christ that he can truly understand the Lord's will and consequently his own vocation.

The better you know Jesus, the more his mystery attracts you. The more you discover him, the more you are moved to seek him. This is a movement of the Spirit which lasts throughout life and which makes the seminary a time of immense promise, a true "springtime".

When the Magi came to Bethlehem, "going into the house they saw the child with Mary his mother, and they fell down and worshipped him" (Mt 2:11). Here at last was the long-awaited moment: their encounter with Jesus.

"Going into the house": this house in some sense represents the Church. In order to find the Savior, one has to enter the house, which is the Church.

During his time in the seminary, a particularly important process of maturation takes place in the consciousness of the young seminarian: he no longer sees the Church "from the outside", but rather, as it were, "from the inside", and he comes to sense that she is his "home", inasmuch as she is the home of Christ, where "Mary his mother" dwells.

It is Mary who shows him Jesus her Son; she introduces him and in a sense enables him to see and touch Jesus and to take him into his arms. Mary teaches the seminarian to contemplate Jesus with the eyes of the heart and to make Jesus his very life.

Each moment of seminary life can be an opportunity for loving experience of the presence of Our Lady, who introduces everyone to an encounter with Christ in the silence of meditation, prayer and fraternity. Mary helps us to meet the Lord above all in the celebration of the Eucharist, when, in the Word and in the consecrated Bread, he becomes our daily spiritual nourishment.

"They fell down and worshipped him . . . and offered him gifts: gold, frankincense and myrrh" (Mt 2:11–12). Here is the culmination of the whole journey: encounter becomes adoration; it blossoms into an act of faith and love which acknowledges in Jesus, born of Mary, the Son of God made man.

How can we fail to see prefigured in this gesture of the Magi the faith of Simon Peter and of the other apostles, the faith of Paul and of all the saints, particularly of the many saintly seminarians and priests who have graced the 2,000 years of the Church's history?

The secret of holiness is friendship with Christ and faithful obedience to his will. Saint Ambrose said: "Christ is everything for us"; and Saint Benedict warned against putting anything before the love of Christ.

May Christ be everything for you. Dear seminarians, be the first to offer him what is most precious to you, as Pope John Paul II suggested in his *Message for this World Youth Day*: the gold of your freedom, the incense of your ardent prayer, the myrrh of your most profound affection (cf. no. 4).

The seminary years are a time of preparing for mission. The Magi "departed for their own country" and most certainly bore witness to their encounter with the King of the Jews.

You too, after your long, necessary program of seminary formation, will be sent forth as ministers of Christ; indeed, each of you will return as an *alter Christus*.

On their homeward journey, the Magi surely had to deal with dangers, weariness, disorientation, doubts. The star was no longer there to guide them! The light was now within them. Their task was to guard and nourish it in the constant memory of Christ, of his Holy Face, of his ineffable Love.

Dear seminarians! One day, God willing, by the consecration of the Holy Spirit you too will begin your mission. Remember always the words of Jesus: "Abide in my love" (Jn 15:9). If you abide close to Christ, with Christ and in Christ, you will bear much fruit, just as he promised. You have not chosen him—we have just heard this in the witnesses given— he has chosen you (cf. Jn 15:16).

Here is the secret of your vocation and your mission! It is kept in the Immaculate Heart of Mary, who watches over each one of you with a mother's love. Have recourse to Mary, often and with confidence.

I assure you of my affection and my daily prayers. And I bless all of you from my heart.

YOUTH VIGIL

Dear Young Friends,

In our pilgrimage with the mysterious Magi from the East, we have arrived at the moment which Saint Matthew describes in his Gospel with these words: "Going into the house (over which the star had halted), they saw the child with Mary his mother, and they fell down and worshipped him" (Mt 2:11). Outwardly, their journey was now over. They had reached their goal.

But at this point a new journey began for them, an inner pilgrimage which changed their whole lives. Their mental picture of the infant King they were expecting to find must have been very different. They had stopped at Jerusalem specifically in order to ask the King who lived there for news of the promised King who had been born. They knew that the world was in disorder, and for that reason their hearts were troubled.

They were sure that God existed and that he was a just and gentle God. And perhaps they also knew of the great prophecies of Israel foretelling a King who would be intimately united with God, a King who would restore order to the world, acting for God and in his Name.

It was in order to seek this King that they had set off on their journey: deep within themselves they felt prompted to go in search of the true justice that can only come from God, and they wanted to serve this King, to fall prostrate at his feet and so play their part in the renewal of the world. They were among those "who hunger and thirst for justice" (Mt 5:6). This hunger and thirst had spurred them on in their pilgrimage—they had become pilgrims in search of the justice that they expected from God, intending to devote themselves to its service.

Even if those who had stayed at home may have considered them Utopian dreamers, they were actually people with their feet on the ground, and they knew that in order to change the world it is necessary to have power. Hence, they were hardly likely to seek the promised child anywhere but in the King's palace. Yet now they were bowing down before the child of poor people, and they soon came to realize that Herod, the King they had consulted, intended to use his power to lay a trap for him, forcing the family to flee into exile.

The new King, to whom they now paid homage, was quite unlike what they were expecting. In this way they had to learn that God is not as we usually imagine him to be. This was where their inner journey began. It started at the very moment when they knelt down before this child and recognized him as the promised King. But they still had to assimilate these joyful gestures internally.

They had to change their ideas about power, about God and about man, and in so doing, they also had to change themselves. Now they were able to see that God's power is not like that of the powerful of this world. God's ways are not as we imagine them or as we might wish them to be.

God does not enter into competition with earthly powers in this world. He does not marshal his divisions alongside other divisions. God did not send twelve legions of angels to assist Jesus in the Garden of Olives (cf. Mt 26:53). He contrasts the noisy and ostentatious power of this world with the defenseless power of love, which succumbs to death on the Cross and dies ever anew throughout history; yet it is this same love which constitutes the new divine intervention that opposes injustice and ushers in the Kingdom of God.

God is different—this is what they now come to realize.

And it means that they themselves must now become different, they must learn God's ways.

They had come to place themselves at the service of this King, to model their own kingship on his. That was the meaning of their act of homage, their adoration. Included in this were their gifts—gold, frankincense and myrrh—gifts offered to a King held to be divine. Adoration has a content and it involves giving. Through this act of adoration, these men from the East wished to recognize the child as their King and to place their own power and potential at his disposal, and in this they were certainly on the right path.

By serving and following him, they wanted, together with him, to serve the cause of good and the cause of justice in the world. In this they were right.

Now, though, they have to learn that this cannot be achieved simply through issuing commands from a throne on high. Now they have to learn to give themselves—no lesser gift would be sufficient for this King. Now they have to learn that their lives must be conformed to this divine way of exercising power, to God's own way of being.

They must become men of truth, of justice, of goodness, of forgiveness, of mercy. They will no longer ask: How can this serve me? Instead, they will have to ask: How can I serve God's presence in the world? They must learn to lose their life and in this way to find it. Having left Jerusalem behind, they must not deviate from the path marked out by the true King, as they follow Jesus.

Dear friends, what does all this mean for us?

What we have just been saying about the nature of God being different, and about the way our lives must be shaped accordingly, sounds very fine, but remains rather vague and unfocused. That is why God has given us examples. The Magi from the East are just the first in a long procession of men and women who have constantly tried to gaze upon God's star in their lives, going in search of the God who has drawn close to us and shows us the way.

It is the great multitude of the saints—both known and unknown—in whose lives the Lord has opened up the Gospel before us and turned over the pages; he has done this throughout history and he still does so today. In their lives, as if in a great picture-book, the riches of the Gospel are revealed. They are the shining path which God himself has traced throughout history and is still tracing today.

My venerable Predecessor Pope John Paul II, who is with us at this moment, beatified and canonized a great many people from both the distant and the recent past. Through these individuals he wanted to show us how to be Christian: how to live life as it should be lived—according to God's way. The saints and the blesseds did not doggedly seek their own happiness, but simply wanted to give themselves, because the light of Christ had shone upon them.

They show us the way to attain happiness; they show us how to be truly human. Through all the ups and downs of history, they were the true reformers who constantly rescued it from plunging into the valley of darkness; it was they who constantly shed upon it the light that was needed to make sense— even in the midst of suffering—of God's words spoken at the end of the work of creation: "It is very good."

One need only think of such figures as Saint Benedict, Saint Francis of Assisi, Saint Teresa of Avila, Saint Ignatius of Loyola, Saint Charles Borromeo, the founders of nineteenth-century religious orders who inspired and guided the social movement, or the saints of our own day—Maximilian Kolbe, Edith Stein, Mother Teresa, Padre Pio. In contemplating these figures we learn what it means "to adore" and what it means to live according to the measure of the Child of Bethlehem, by the measure of Jesus Christ and of God himself.

The saints, as we said, are the true reformers. Now I want to express this in an even more radical way: only from the saints, only from God does true revolution come, the definitive way to change the world.

In the last century we experienced revolutions with a

common program—expecting nothing more from God, they assumed total responsibility for the cause of the world in order to change it. And this, as we saw, meant that a human and partial point of view was always taken as an absolute guiding principle. Absolutizing what is not absolute but relative is called totalitarianism. It does not liberate man, but takes away his dignity and enslaves him.

It is not ideologies that save the world, but only a return to the living God, our Creator, the guarantor of our freedom, the guarantor of what is really good and true. True revolution consists in simply turning to God, who is the measure of what is right and who at the same time is everlasting love. And what could ever save us apart from love?

Dear friends! Allow me to add just two brief thoughts.

There are many who speak of God; some even preach hatred and perpetrate violence in God's Name. So it is important to discover the true face of God. The Magi from the East found it when they knelt down before the Child of Bethlehem. "Anyone who has seen me has seen the Father", said Jesus to Philip (Jn 14:9). In Jesus Christ, who allowed his heart to be pierced for us, the true face of God is seen. We will follow him together with the great multitude of those who went before us. Then we will be traveling along the right path.

This means that we are not constructing a private God, we are not constructing a private Jesus, but that we believe and worship the Jesus who is manifested to us by the Sacred Scriptures and who reveals himself to be alive in the great procession of the faithful called the Church, always alongside us and always before us.

There is much that could be criticized in the Church. We know this and the Lord himself told us so: it is a net with good fish and bad fish, a field with wheat and darnel.

Pope John Paul II, as well as revealing the true face of the Church in the many saints that he canonized, also asked pardon for the wrong that was done in the course of history through the words and deeds of members of the Church. In this way he showed us our own true image and urged us to take our place, with all our faults and weaknesses, in the procession of the saints that began with the Magi from the East.

It is actually consoling to realize that there is darnel in the Church. In this way, despite all our defects, we can still hope to be counted among the disciples of Jesus, who came to call sinners.

The Church is like a human family, but at the same time she is also the great family of God, through which he establishes an overarching communion and unity that embraces every continent, culture and nation. So we are glad to belong to this great family that we see here; we are glad to have brothers and friends all over the world.

Here in Cologne we discover the joy of belonging to a family as vast as the world, including Heaven and earth, the past, the present, the future and every part of the earth. In this great band of pilgrims we walk side by side with Christ, we walk with the star that enlightens our history.

"Going into the house, they saw the child with Mary his mother, and they fell down and worshipped him" (Mt 2:11). Dear friends, this is not a distant story that took place long ago. It is with us now. Here in the Sacred Host he is present before us and in our midst. As at that time, so now he is mysteriously veiled in a sacred silence; as at that time, it is here that the true face of God is revealed. For us he became a grain of wheat that falls on the ground and dies and bears fruit until the end of the world (cf. Jn 12:24).

He is present now as he was then in Bethlehem. He invites us to that inner pilgrimage which is called adoration. Let us set off on this pilgrimage of the spirit, and let us ask him to be our guide. Amen.

EUCHARISTIC CELEBRATION

HOMILY OF HIS HOLINESS POPE BENEDICT XVI

COLOGNE—MARIENFELD / SUNDAY, 21 AUGUST 2005

(BEFORE THE MASS)

Dear Cardinal Meisner,
Dear Young People,

I would like to thank you, dear Confrère in the Episcopate, for the touching words you have addressed to me which introduced us so appropriately into the Eucharistic celebration.

I would have liked to tour the hill in the Popemobile and to be closer to each one of you, individually. Unfortunately, this has proved impossible, but I greet each one of you from the bottom of my heart. The Lord sees and loves each individual person, and we are all the living Church for one another, and let us thank God for this moment in which he is giving us the gift of the mystery of his presence and the possibility of being in communion with him.

We all know that we are imperfect, that we are unable to be a fitting house for him. Let us therefore begin Holy Mass by meditating and praying to him, so that he will take from us what divides us from him and what separates us from each other and enable us to become familiar with the holy mysteries.

Dear Young Friends,

Yesterday evening we came together in the presence of the Sacred Host, in which Jesus becomes for us the bread that sustains and feeds us (cf. Jn 6:35), and there we began our inner journey of adoration. In the Eucharist, adoration must become union.

At the celebration of the Eucharist, we find ourselves in the "hour" of Jesus, to use the language of John's Gospel. Through the Eucharist this "hour" of Jesus becomes our own hour, his presence in our midst. Together with the disciples he celebrated the Passover of Israel, the memorial of God's liberating action that led Israel from slavery to freedom. Jesus follows the rites of Israel. He recites over the bread the prayer of praise and blessing.

But then something new happens. He thanks God not only for the great works of the past; he thanks him for his own exaltation, soon to be accomplished through the Cross and Resurrection, and he speaks to the disciples in words that sum up the whole of the Law and the Prophets: "This is my Body, given in sacrifice for you. This cup is the New Covenant in my Blood." He then distributes the bread and the cup, and instructs them to repeat his words and actions of that moment over and over again in his memory.

What is happening? How can Jesus distribute his Body and his Blood?

By making the bread into his Body and the wine into his Blood, he anticipates his death, he accepts it in his heart, and he transforms it into an action of love. What on the outside is simply brutal violence—the Crucifixion—from within becomes an act of total self-giving love. This is the substantial transformation which was accomplished at the Last Supper and was destined to set in motion a series of transformations leading ultimately to the transformation of the world when God will be all in all (cf. 1 Cor 15:28).

In their hearts, people always and everywhere have somehow expected a change, a transformation of the world. Here now is the central act of transformation that alone can truly renew the world: violence is transformed into love, and death into life.

Since this act transmutes death into love, death as such is already conquered from within, the Resurrection is already present in it. Death is, so to speak, mortally wounded, so that it can no longer have the last word.

To use an image well known to us today, this is like inducing nuclear fission in the very heart of being—the victory of love over hatred, the victory of love over death. Only this intimate explosion of good conquering evil can then trigger off the series of transformations that little by little will change the world.

All other changes remain superficial and cannot save. For this reason we speak of redemption: what had to happen at the most intimate level has indeed happened, and we can enter into its dynamic. Jesus can distribute his Body, because he truly gives himself.

This first fundamental transformation of violence into love, of death into life, brings other changes in its wake. Bread and wine become his Body and Blood.

But it must not stop there; on the contrary, the process of transformation must now gather momentum. The Body and Blood of Christ are given to us so that we ourselves will be transformed in our turn. We are to become the Body of Christ, his own Flesh and Blood.

We all eat the one bread, and this means that we ourselves become one. In this way, adoration, as we said earlier, becomes union. God no longer simply stands before us as the One who is totally Other. He is within us, and we are in him. His dynamic enters into us and then seeks to spread outwards to others until it fills the world, so that his love can truly become the dominant measure of the world.

I like to illustrate this new step urged upon us by the Last Supper by drawing out the different nuances of the word "adoration" in Greek and in Latin. The Greek word is *proskynesis*. It refers to the gesture of submission, the recognition of God as our true measure, supplying the norm that we choose to follow. It means that freedom is not simply about enjoying life in total autonomy, but rather about living by the measure of truth and goodness, so that we ourselves can become true and good. This gesture is necessary even if initially our yearning for freedom makes us inclined to resist it.

We can fully accept it only when we take the second step that the Last Supper proposes to us. The Latin word for adoration is *ad-oratio*—mouth to mouth contact, a kiss, an embrace, and hence, ultimately love. Submission becomes union, because he to whom we submit is Love. In this way submission acquires a meaning, because it does not impose anything on us from the outside, but liberates us deep within.

Let us return once more to the Last Supper. The new element to emerge here was the deeper meaning given to Israel's ancient prayer of blessing, which from that point on became the word of transformation, enabling us to participate in the "hour" of Christ. Jesus did not instruct us to repeat the Passover meal, which in any event, given that it is an anniversary, is not repeatable at will. He instructed us to enter into his "hour".

We enter into it through the sacred power of the words of consecration—a transformation brought about through the prayer of praise which places us in continuity with Israel and the whole of salvation history and at the same time ushers in the new, to which the older prayer at its deepest level was pointing.

The new prayer—which the Church calls the "Eucharistic Prayer"—brings the Eucharist into being. It is the word of power which transforms the gifts of the earth in an entirely new way into God's gift of himself, and it draws us into this process of transformation. That is why we call this action "Eucharist", which is a translation of the Hebrew word *beracha*—thanksgiving, praise, blessing, and a transformation worked by the Lord: the presence of his "hour". Jesus' hour is the hour in which love triumphs. In other words: it is God who has triumphed, because he is Love.

Jesus' hour seeks to become our own hour and will indeed

become so if we allow ourselves, through the celebration of the Eucharist, to be drawn into that process of transformation that the Lord intends to bring about. The Eucharist must become the center of our lives.

If the Church tells us that the Eucharist is an essential part of Sunday, this is no mere positivism or thirst for power. On Easter morning, first the women and then the disciples had the grace of seeing the Lord. From that moment on, they knew that the first day of the week, Sunday, would be his day, the day of Christ the Lord. The day when creation began became the day when creation was renewed. Creation and redemption belong together. That is why Sunday is so important.

It is good that today, in many cultures, Sunday is a free day and is often combined with Saturday so as to constitute a "week-end" of free time. Yet this free time is empty if God is not present.

Dear friends! Sometimes, our initial impression is that having to include time for Mass on a Sunday is rather inconvenient. But if you make the effort, you will realize that this is what gives a proper focus to your free time.

Do not be deterred from taking part in Sunday Mass, and help others to discover it too. This is because the Eucharist releases the joy that we need so much, and we must learn to grasp it ever more deeply, we must learn to love it.

Let us pledge ourselves to do this—it is worth the effort! Let us discover the intimate riches of the Church's liturgy and its true greatness: it is not we who are celebrating for ourselves, but it is the living God himself who is preparing a banquet for us.

Through your love for the Eucharist you will also rediscover the Sacrament of Reconciliation, in which the merciful goodness of God always allows us to make a fresh start in our lives.

Anyone who has discovered Christ must lead others to him. A great joy cannot be kept to oneself. It has to be passed on.

In vast areas of the world today there is a strange forgetfulness of God. It seems as if everything would be just the same even without him.

But at the same time there is a feeling of frustration, a sense of dissatisfaction with everyone and everything.

People tend to exclaim: "This cannot be what life is about!" Indeed not. And so, together with forgetfulness of God there is a kind of new explosion of religion. I have no wish to discredit all the manifestations of this phenomenon. There may be sincere joy in the discovery. But to tell the truth, religion often becomes almost a consumer product. People choose what they like, and some are even able to make a profit from it.

But religion sought on a "do-it-yourself" basis cannot ultimately help us. It may be comfortable, but at times of crisis we are left to ourselves.

Help people to discover the true star which points out the way to us: Jesus Christ! Let us seek to know him better and better, so as to be able to guide others to him with conviction.

This is why love for Sacred Scripture is so important, and, in consequence, it is important to know the faith of the Church which opens up for us the meaning of Scripture. It is the Holy Spirit who guides the Church as her faith grows, causing her to enter ever more deeply into the truth (cf. Jn 16:13).

Beloved Pope John Paul II gave us a wonderful work in which the faith of centuries is explained synthetically: the *Catechism of the Catholic Church*. I myself recently presented the *Compendium* of the *Catechism*, also prepared at the request of the late Holy Father. These are two fundamental texts which I recommend to all of you.

Obviously books alone are not enough. Form communities based on faith!

In recent decades, movements and communities have come to birth in which the power of the Gospel is keenly felt. Seek communion in faith, like fellow travelers who continue together to follow the path of the great pilgrimage that the Magi from the East first pointed out to us. The spontaneity of new communities is important, but it is also important to preserve communion with the Pope and with the Bishops. It is they who guarantee that we are not seeking private paths, but instead are living as God's great family, founded by the Lord through the twelve apostles.

Once again, I must return to the Eucharist. "Because there is one bread, we, though many, are one body", says Saint Paul (1 Cor 10:17). By this he meant: since we receive the same Lord and he gathers us together and draws us into himself, we ourselves are one.

This must be evident in our lives. It must be seen in our capacity to forgive. It must be seen in our sensitivity to the needs of others. It must be seen in our willingness to share. It must be seen in our commitment to our neighbors, both those close at hand and those physically far away, whom we nevertheless consider to be close.

Today, there are many forms of voluntary assistance, models of mutual service, of which our society has urgent need. We must not, for example, abandon the elderly to their solitude; we must not pass by when we meet people who are suffering. If we think and live according to our communion with Christ, then our eyes will be opened. Then we will no longer be content to scrape a living just for ourselves, but we will see where and how we are needed.

Living and acting thus, we will soon realize that it is much better to be useful and at the disposal of others than to be concerned only with the comforts that are offered to us.

I know that you as young people have great aspirations, that you want to pledge yourselves to build a better world. Let others see this, let the world see it, since this is exactly the witness that the world expects from the disciples of Jesus Christ; in this way, and through your love above all, the world will be able to discover the star that we follow as believers.

Let us go forward with Christ and let us live our lives as true worshippers of God! Amen.

ANGELUS

BENEDICT XVI

COLOGNE—MARIENFELD / SUNDAY, 21 AUGUST 2005

Dear Friends,

We have come to the conclusion of this marvelous celebration and indeed of the *Twentieth World Youth Day*. In my heart I sense welling up within me a single thought: "Thank you!" I am sure—and I feel—that this thought finds an echo in each one of you. God himself has implanted it in our hearts, and he has sealed it with this Eucharist, which literally means "thanksgiving".

Yes, dear young people, our gratitude, born from faith, is expressed in our song of praise to him, Father, Son and Holy Spirit, who has offered to us a great sign of his immense love.

Our "thank you", to begin with, rises up to God—only he could have given it to us in this way, as it was—and our thanks are now extended to all those who have been involved in its preparation and organization.

World Youth Day was a gift, but, as it developed, it was also the result of much work. For this I must renew my gratitude particularly to the Pontifical Council for the Laity, under its President Archbishop Stanisław Ryłko, ably assisted by the Secretary, Bishop Josef Clemens, who for years was my Secretary, and also to my Confrères from the German Bishops' Conference, in the first place, of course, to the Archbishop of Cologne, Cardinal Joachim Meisner. I am grateful to the political and administrative Authorities, who have made a great contribution, who have generously helped and who have ensured that each event has run smoothly.

In a particular way I thank the many volunteers from all of the German Dioceses and from all the nations. A cordial word of thanks goes also to the many contemplative communities who have supported us in prayer during this World Youth Day.

And now, as the living presence of the Risen Christ in our midst nourishes our faith and hope, I am pleased to announce that the next World Youth Day will take place in Sydney, Australia, in 2008. We entrust to the maternal guidance of Mary Most Holy the future course of the young people of the whole world. Let us now recite the *Angelus*.

Angelus Domini . . .

(AFTER THE ANGELUS)

[*French*] I greet affectionately the French-speaking young people. Thank you, dear friends, for your participation, and I trust that you return home bringing within you, like the Magi, the joy of having found Christ, the Son of the living God.

[*English*] I extend a warm greeting to the English-speaking young people from all parts of the world at the conclusion of these unforgettable days. May the light of Christ, which you have followed on your way to Cologne, shine ever more brightly and strongly in your lives!

[*Spanish*] Dear Spanish-speaking young people! You have come to worship Christ. Now that you have found him, continue to worship him in your hearts, always prepared to make a defense to any one who calls you to account for the hope that is in you (cf. 1 Pet 3:15). Have a pleasant return home!

[*Italian*] My dear Italian-speaking friends! This Twentieth World Youth Day is ending, but the Eucharistic celebration must continue in our lives: bring to all the joy of Christ that you have found here.

[*Polish*] To all the young Polish people, I extend a warm embrace! As the great Pope John Paul II would say: keep the flame of faith alive in your lives and in your people. May Our Lady, Mother of Christ, guide your steps always.

[*Portuguese*] I greet with affection the Portuguese-speaking young people. I pray, dear friends, that you will always live in friendship with Jesus, so as to know true joy and communicate it to others, especially to young people in difficulty.

[*Tagalog*] My dear Tagalog-speaking friends and all the young people of Asia! Like the Magi, you too have come from the East to worship Christ. Now that you have found him, return to your countries bringing in your hearts the light of his love.

[*Swahili*] A warm greeting also to you, young people from Africa! Bring to your great and beloved Continent the hope that Christ has given you. Be everywhere sowers of peace and brotherhood.

[*German*] Dear friends who understand me in my own language, I thank you for the affection with which you have sustained me in these days. Be close to me in prayer. Walk together in unity. Always be faithful to Christ and to the Church. May the peace and the joy of Christ be with you always!

Interreligious Dialogue

VISIT TO THE SYNAGOGUE OF COLOGNE

ADDRESS OF HIS HOLINESS POPE BENEDICT XVI

COLOGNE—SYNAGOGUE / FRIDAY, 19 AUGUST 2005

Distinguished Jewish Authorities, Ladies and Gentlemen,
Dear Brothers and Sisters,

I greet all those who have already been mentioned. *Shalom lêchém!*

It has been my deep desire, during my first Visit to Germany since my election as the Successor of the apostle Peter, to meet the Jewish community of Cologne and the representatives of Judaism in Germany. By this Visit I would like to return in spirit to the meeting that took place in Mainz on 17 November 1980 between my venerable Predecessor Pope John Paul II, then making *his first Visit to this Country*, and members of the Central Jewish Committee in Germany and the Rabbinic Conference.

Today, too, I wish to reaffirm that I intend to continue with great vigor on the path towards improved relations and friendship with the Jewish People, following the decisive lead given by Pope John Paul II (cf. *Address to the Delegation of the International Jewish Committee on Interreligious Consultations*, 9 June 2005).

The Jewish community in Cologne can truly feel "at home" in this city. Cologne is, in fact, the oldest site of a Jewish community on German soil, dating back to the Colonia of Roman times, as we have come to know with precision.

The history of relations between the Jewish and Christian communities has been complex and often painful. There were blessed times when the two lived together peacefully, but there was also the expulsion of the Jews from Cologne in the year 1424.

And in the twentieth century, in the darkest period of German and European history, an insane racist ideology, born of neo-paganism, gave rise to the attempt, planned and systematically carried out by the regime, to exterminate European Jewry. The result has passed into history as the *Shoah*.

The victims of this unspeakable and previously unimaginable crime amounted to 11,000 named individuals in Cologne alone; the real figure was surely much higher. The holiness of God was no longer recognized, and, consequently, contempt was shown for the sacredness of human life.

This year, 2005, marks the sixtieth anniversary of the liberation of the Nazi concentration camps, in which millions of Jews—men, women and children—were put to death in the gas chambers and ovens.

I make my own the words written by my venerable Predecessor on the occasion of the sixtieth anniversary of the liberation of Auschwitz, and I too say: "I bow my head before all those who experienced this manifestation of the *mysterium iniquitatis*." The terrible events of that time must "never cease to rouse consciences, to resolve conflicts, to inspire the building of peace" (*Message for the Liberation of Auschwitz*, 15 January 2005).

Together we must remember God and his wise plan for the world he created. As we read in the Book of Wisdom, he is the "lover of life" (11:26).

This year also marks the fortieth anniversary of the promulgation of the Second Vatican Council's Declaration *Nostra Aetate*, which opened up new prospects for Jewish-Christian relations in terms of dialogue and solidarity. This Declaration, in the fourth chapter, recalls the common roots and the immensely rich spiritual heritage that Jews and Christians share.

Both Jews and Christians recognize in Abraham their father in faith (cf. Gal 3:7; Rom 4:11ff.), and they look to the teachings of Moses and the Prophets. Jewish spirituality, like its

Christian counterpart, draws nourishment from the psalms. With Saint Paul, Christians are convinced that "the gifts and the call of God are irrevocable" (Rom 11:29; cf. 9:6, 11; 11:1ff.). In considering the Jewish roots of Christianity (cf. Rom 11:16–24), my venerable Predecessor, quoting a statement by the German Bishops, affirmed that "whoever meets Jesus Christ meets Judaism" (*Insegnamenti*, vol. III/2, 1980, p. 1272).

The conciliar Declaration *Nostra Aetate* therefore "deplores feelings of hatred, persecutions and demonstrations of anti-Semitism directed against the Jews at whatever time and by whomsoever" (no. 4). God created us all "in his image" (cf. Gen 1:27) and thus honored us with a transcendent dignity. Before God, all men and women have the same dignity, whatever their nation, culture or religion.

Hence, the Declaration *Nostra Aetate* also speaks with great esteem of Muslims (cf. no. 3) and of the followers of other religions (cf. no. 2).

On the basis of our shared human dignity the Catholic Church "condemns as foreign to the mind of Christ any kind of discrimination whatsoever between people, or harassment of them, done by reason of race or color, class or religion" (no. 5).

The Church is conscious of her duty to transmit this teaching, in her catechesis for young people and in every aspect of her life, to the younger generations which did not witness the terrible events that took place before and during the Second World War.

It is a particularly important task, since today, sadly, we are witnessing the rise of new signs of anti-Semitism and various forms of a general hostility towards foreigners. How can we fail to see in this a reason for concern and vigilance?

The Catholic Church is committed—I reaffirm this again today—to tolerance, respect, friendship and peace between all peoples, cultures and religions.

In the forty years that have passed since the conciliar Declaration *Nostra Aetate*, much progress has been made, in Germany and throughout the world, towards better and closer relations between Jews and Christians. Alongside official relationships, due above all to cooperation between specialists in the biblical sciences, many friendships have been born.

In this regard, I would mention the various declarations by the German Episcopal Conference and the charitable work done by the "Society for Jewish-Christian Cooperation in Cologne", which since 1945 have enabled the Jewish community to feel once again truly "at home" here in Cologne and to establish good relations with the Christian communities.

Yet much still remains to be done. We must come to know one another much more and much better.

Consequently, I would encourage sincere and trustful dialogue between Jews and Christians, for only in this way will it be possible to arrive at a shared interpretation of disputed historical questions and, above all, to make progress towards a theological evaluation of the relationship between Judaism and Christianity.

This dialogue, if it is to be sincere, must not gloss over or underestimate the existing differences: in those areas in which, due to our profound convictions in faith, we diverge, and indeed, precisely in those areas, we need to show respect and love for one another.

Finally, our gaze should not only be directed to the past, but should also look forward to the tasks that await us today and tomorrow. Our rich common heritage and our fraternal and more trusting relations call upon us to join in giving an ever more harmonious witness and to work together on the practical level for the defense and promotion of human rights and the sacredness of human life, for family values, for social justice and for peace in the world.

The Decalogue (cf. Ex 20; Deut 5) is for us a shared legacy and commitment. The Ten Commandments are not a burden, but a signpost showing the path leading to a successful life.

This is particularly the case for the young people whom I am meeting in these days and who are so dear to me. My wish is that they may be able to recognize in the Decalogue our common foundation, a lamp for their steps, a light for their path (cf. Ps 119:105).

Adults have the responsibility of handing down to young people the torch of hope that God has given to Jews and to Christians, so that "never again" will the forces of evil come to power and that future generations, with God's help, may be able to build a more just and peaceful world, in which all people have equal rights and are equally at home.

I conclude with the words of Psalm 29, which express both a wish and a prayer: "May the Lord give strength to his people, may he bless his people with peace."

May he hear our prayer!

MEETING WITH REPRESENTATIVES
OF SOME MUSLIM COMMUNITIES

ADDRESS OF HIS HOLINESS POPE BENEDICT XVI

COLOGNE / SATURDAY, 20 AUGUST 2005

Dear Muslim Friends,

It gives me great joy to be able to be with you and to offer you
my heartfelt greetings.

As you know, I have come here to meet young people from
every part of Europe and the world. Young people are the
future of humanity and the hope of the nations. My beloved
Predecessor, *Pope John Paul II, once said to the young Muslims
assembled in the stadium at Casablanca, Morocco: "The young can
build a better future if they first put their faith in God and if they
pledge themselves to build this new world in accordance with God's
plan, with wisdom and trust"* (*Insegnamenti*, VIII/2, 1985, p. 500).

It is in this spirit that I turn to you, dear and esteemed
Muslim friends, to share my hopes with you and to let you
know of my concerns at these particularly difficult times in our
history.

I am certain that I echo your own thoughts when I bring up
one of our concerns as we notice the spread of terrorism. I
know that many of you have firmly rejected, also publicly, in
particular any connection between your faith and terrorism
and have condemned it. I am grateful to you for this, for it
contributes to the climate of trust that we need.

Terrorist activity is continually recurring in various parts of
the world, plunging people into grief and despair. Those who
instigate and plan these attacks evidently wish to poison our
relations and destroy trust, making use of all means, including

religion, to oppose every attempt to build a peaceful and serene life together.

Thanks be to God, we agree on the fact that terrorism of any kind is a perverse and cruel choice which shows contempt for the sacred right to life and undermines the very foundations of all civil coexistence.

If together we can succeed in eliminating from hearts any trace of rancor, in resisting every form of intolerance and in opposing every manifestation of violence, we will turn back the wave of cruel fanaticism that endangers the lives of so many people and hinders progress towards world peace.

The task is difficult but not impossible. The believer—and all of us, as Christians and Muslims, are believers—knows that, despite his weakness, he can count on the spiritual power of prayer.

Dear friends, I am profoundly convinced that we must not yield to the negative pressures in our midst, but must affirm the values of mutual respect, solidarity and peace. The life of every human being is sacred, both for Christians and for Muslims. There is plenty of scope for us to act together in the service of fundamental moral values.

The dignity of the person and the defense of the rights which that dignity confers must represent the goal of every social endeavor and of every effort to bring it to fruition. This message is conveyed to us unmistakably by the quiet but clear voice of conscience. It is a message which must be heeded and communicated to others: should it ever cease to find an echo in peoples' hearts, the world would be exposed to the darkness of a new barbarism.

Only through recognition of the centrality of the person can a common basis for understanding be found, one which enables us to move beyond cultural conflicts and which neutralizes the disruptive power of ideologies.

During my *Meeting last April with the delegates of Churches and Christian Communities and with representatives of the various religious traditions*, I affirmed that "the Church wants to continue building bridges of friendship with the followers of all religions, in order to seek the true good of every person and of society as a whole" (*L'Osservatore Romano*, 25 April 2005, p. 4).

Past experience teaches us that, unfortunately, relations between Christians and Muslims have not always been marked by mutual respect and understanding. How many pages of history record battles and wars that have been waged, with both sides invoking the Name of God, as if fighting and killing the enemy could be pleasing to him. The recollection of these sad events should fill us with shame, for we know only too well what atrocities have been committed in the name of religion.

The lessons of the past must help us to avoid repeating the same mistakes. We must seek paths of reconciliation and learn to live with respect for each other's identity. The defense of religious freedom, in this sense, is a permanent imperative, and respect for minorities is a clear sign of true civilization. In this regard, it is always right to recall what the Fathers of the Second Vatican Council said about relations with Muslims.

"The Church looks upon Muslims with respect. They worship the one God living and subsistent, merciful and almighty, creator of heaven and earth, who has spoken to humanity and to whose decrees, even the hidden ones, they seek to submit themselves whole-heartedly, just as Abraham, to whom the Islamic faith readily relates itself, submitted to God. . . . Although considerable dissensions and enmities between Christians and Muslims may have arisen in the course of the centuries, the Council urges all parties that, forgetting past things, they train themselves towards sincere mutual understanding and together maintain and promote social justice and moral values as well as peace and freedom for all people" (Declaration *Nostra Aetate*, no. 3).

For us, these words of the Second Vatican Council remain the *Magna Carta* of the dialogue with you, dear Muslim friends, and I am glad that you have spoken to us in the same spirit and have confirmed these intentions.

You, my esteemed friends, represent some Muslim communities from this Country where I was born, where I studied and where I lived for a good part of my life. That is why I wanted to meet you. You guide Muslim believers and train them in the Islamic faith.

Teaching is the vehicle through which ideas and convictions are transmitted. Words are highly influential in the education of the mind. You, therefore, have a great responsibility for the formation of the younger generation. I learn with gratitude of the spirit in which you assume this responsibility.

Christians and Muslims, we must face together the many challenges of our time. There is no room for apathy and disengagement, and even less for partiality and sectarianism. We must not yield to fear or pessimism. Rather, we must cultivate optimism and hope.

Interreligious and intercultural dialogue between Christians and Muslims cannot be reduced to an optional extra. It is in fact a vital necessity, on which in large measure our future depends.

The young people from many parts of the world are here in Cologne as living witnesses of solidarity, brotherhood and love.

I pray with all my heart, dear and esteemed Muslim friends, that the merciful and compassionate God may protect you, bless you and enlighten you always.

May the God of peace lift up our hearts, nourish our hope and guide our steps on the paths of the world.

Thank you!

Ecumenical Dialogue

APOSTOLIC JOURNEY TO COLOGNE
ON THE OCCASION OF
THE TWENTIETH WORLD YOUTH DAY

ECUMENICAL MEETING

ADDRESS OF HIS HOLINESS POPE BENEDICT XVI

COLOGNE—ARCHBISHOP'S HOUSE / FRIDAY, 19 AUGUST 2005

Dear Brothers and Sisters,

Permit me to remain seated after such a strenuous day. This does not mean I wish to speak "ex cathedra". Also, excuse me for being late. Unfortunately, Vespers took longer than foreseen, and the traffic was slower moving than could be imagined.

I would like now to express the joy I feel on the occasion of my Visit to Germany, in being able to meet you and offer a warm greeting to you, the Representatives of the other Churches and Ecclesial Communities.

As a native of this Country, I am quite aware of the painful situation which the rupture of unity in the profession of the faith has entailed for so many individuals and families. This was one of the reasons why, immediately following my election as Bishop of Rome, I declared, as the Successor of the apostle Peter, my firm commitment to making the recovery of full and visible Christian unity a priority of my Pontificate.

In doing so, I wished consciously to follow in the footsteps of two of my great Predecessors: Pope Paul VI, who over forty years ago signed the conciliar Decree on Ecumenism *Unitatis Redintegratio*, and Pope John Paul II, who made that Document the inspiration for his activity.

In ecumenical dialogue Germany without a doubt has a place of particular importance. We are the Country where the Reformation began; however, Germany is also one of the countries where the ecumenical movement of the twentieth century originated.

With the successive waves of immigration in the last century, Christians from the Orthodox Churches and the ancient Churches of the East also found a new homeland in this Country. This certainly favored greater contact and exchanges so that now there is a dialogue among the three of us.

Together we can rejoice in the fact that the dialogue, with the passage of time, has brought about a renewed sense of our brotherhood and has created a more open and trusting climate between Christians belonging to the various Churches and Ecclesial Communities. My venerable Predecessor, in his Encyclical *Ut Unum Sint* (1995), saw this as an especially significant fruit of dialogue (cf. nos. 41ff.; 64).

I feel the fact that we consider one another brothers and sisters, that we love one another, that together we are witnesses of Jesus Christ, should not be taken so much for granted. I believe that this brotherhood is in itself a very important fruit of dialogue that we must rejoice in, continue to foster and to practice.

Among Christians, fraternity is not just a vague sentiment, nor is it a sign of indifference to truth. As you just said, Bishop, it is grounded in the supernatural reality of the one Baptism which makes us all members of the one Body of Christ (cf. 1 Cor 12:13; Gal 3:28; Col 2:12).

Together we confess that Jesus Christ is God and Lord; together we acknowledge him as the one mediator between God and man (cf. 1 Tim 2:5), and we emphasize that together we are members of his Body (cf. *Unitatis Redintegratio*, no. 22; *Ut Unum Sint*, no. 42).

Based on this essential foundation of Baptism, a reality comes from him which is a way of being, then of professing, believing and acting. Based on this crucial foundation, dialogue has borne its fruits and will continue to do so.

I would like to mention the re-examination of the mutual condemnations, called for by John Paul II during *his first Visit to Germany*. I recall with some nostalgia that first Visit. I was able to be present when we were together at Mainz in a fairly small and authentic fraternal circle. Some questions were put to the Pope, and he described a broad theological vision in which reciprocity was amply treated.

That colloquium gave rise to an episcopal, that is, a Church commission, under ecclesial responsibility. Finally, with the contribution of theologians it led to the important *Joint Declaration on the Doctrine of Justification* (1999) and to an agreement on basic issues that had been a subject of controversy since the sixteenth century.

We should also acknowledge with gratitude the results of our common stand on important matters, such as the fundamental questions involving the defense of life and the promotion of justice and peace.

I am well aware that many Christians in Germany, and not only in this Country, expect further concrete steps to bring us closer together. I myself have the same expectation.

It is the Lord's commandment, but also the imperative of the present hour, to carry on dialogue with conviction at all levels of the Church's life. This must obviously take place with sincerity and realism, with patience and perseverance, in complete fidelity to the dictates of one's conscience in the awareness that it is the Lord who gives unity, that we do not create it, that it is he who gives it but that we must go to meet him.

I do not intend here to outline a program for the immediate themes of dialogue—this task belongs to theologians working alongside the Bishops: the theologians, on the basis of their knowledge of the problem; the Bishops, from their knowledge of the concrete situation in the Church in our Country and in the world.

May I make a small comment: now, it is said that following the clarification regarding the Doctrine of Justification, the elaboration of ecclesiological issues and the questions concerning ministry are the main obstacles still to be overcome. Ultimately, this is true, but I must also say that I dislike this terminology, which from a certain point of view delimits the problem since it seems that we must now debate about institutions instead of the Word of God, as though we had to place our institutions in the center and fight for them. I think that in this way the ecclesiological issue as well as that of the "ministerium" are not dealt with correctly.

The real question is the presence of the Word in the world. In the second century the early Church primarily took a threefold decision: first, to establish the canon, thereby stressing the sovereignty of the Word and explaining that not only is the Old Testament *"hai graphai"*, but together with the New Testament constitutes a single Scripture and is thus for us the master text.

However, at the same time the Church has formulated an Apostolic Succession, the episcopal ministry, in the awareness that the Word and the witness go together; that is, the Word is alive and present only thanks to the witness, so to speak, and receives from the witness its interpretation. But the witness is only such if he witnesses to the Word.

Third and last, the Church has added the *"regula fidei"* as a key for interpretation. I believe that this reciprocal compenetration constitutes an object of dissent between us, even though we are certainly united on fundamental things.

Therefore, when we speak of ecclesiology and of ministry we should preferably speak about this combination of Word and witness and rule of faith and consider it an ecclesiological question and, at the same time, a question of the Word of God, of his sovereignty and humility, inasmuch as the Lord entrusts his Word to witnesses and concedes its interpretation, which, however, must always be measured against the *"regula fidei"* and the integrity of the Word. Excuse me if I have expressed a personal opinion; it seemed right to do so.

Another urgent priority in ecumenical dialogue arises from the great ethical questions of our time; in this area, contemporary man, who is searching, rightly expects a common response on the part of Christians, which, thanks be to God, in many cases has been forthcoming.

There are so many common declarations by the German Bishops' Conference and the Evangelical Churches in Germany that we can be grateful for, but, unfortunately, this does not always happen. Because of contradictory positions in this area our witness to the Gospel and the ethical guidance which we owe to the faithful and to society lose their impact and often appear too vague, with the result that we fail in our duty to provide the witness that is needed in our time.

Our divisions are contrary to the will of Jesus, and they disappoint peoples' expectations. I think that we must work with new energy and dedication to bring a common witness into the context of these great ethical challenges of our time.

We all know there are numerous models of unity, and you know that the Catholic Church also has as her goal the full visible unity of the disciples of Christ, as defined by the Second Vatican Ecumenical Council in its various Documents (cf. *Lumen Gentium*, nos. 8, 13; *Unitatis Redintegratio*, nos. 2, 4, etc.). This unity, we are convinced, indeed subsists in the Catholic Church, without the possibility of ever being lost (cf. *Unitatis Redintegratio*, no. 4); the Church in fact has not totally disappeared from the world.

On the other hand, this unity does not mean what could be called an ecumenism of return: that is, to deny and to reject one's own faith history. Absolutely not!

It does not mean uniformity in all expressions of theology and spirituality, in liturgical forms and in discipline. Unity in multiplicity, and multiplicity in unity: in my *Homily for the Solemnity of Saints Peter and Paul on 29 June last*, I insisted that full unity and true catholicity in the original sense of the word go together. As a necessary condition for the achievement of this coexistence, the commitment to unity must be constantly purified and renewed; it must constantly grow and mature.

To this end, dialogue has its own contribution to make. More than an exchange of thoughts, an academic exercise, it is an exchange of gifts (cf. *Ut Unum Sint*, no. 28), in which the Churches and the Ecclesial Communities can make available their own riches (cf. *Lumen Gentium*, nos. 8, 15; *Unitatis Redintegratio*, nos. 3, 14ff.; *Ut Unum Sint*, nos. 10–14).

As a result of this commitment, the journey can move forward, step by step, as the Letter to the Ephesians says, until at last we will all "attain to the unity of faith and of the knowledge of the Son of God, to mature manhood, to the measure of the stature of the fullness of Christ" (Eph 4:13).

It is obvious that this dialogue can develop only in a context of sincere and committed spirituality. We cannot "bring about" unity by our powers alone. We can only obtain unity as a gift of the Holy Spirit. Consequently, spiritual ecumenism— prayer, conversion and the sanctification of life—constitutes the heart of the ecumenical encounter and movement (cf. *Unitatis Redintegratio*, no. 8; *Ut Unum Sint*, nos. 15ff., 21, etc.). It could be said that the best form of ecumenism consists in living in accordance with the Gospel.

I would also like in this context to remember the great pioneer of unity, Bro. Roger Schutz, who was so tragically snatched from life. I had known him personally for a long time and had a cordial friendship with him.

He often came to visit me, and, as I already said in Rome on the day of his assassination, I received a letter from him that moved my heart, because in it he emphasized that he was journeying along with me and announced to me that he wanted to come and see me. He is now visiting us and speaking to us from on high. I think that we must listen to him, from within we must listen to his spiritually lived ecumenism and allow ourselves to be led by his witness towards an interiorized and spiritualized ecumenism.

I see good reason in this context for optimism in the fact that today a kind of "network" of spiritual links is developing between Catholics and Christians from the different Churches and Ecclesial Communities: each individual commits himself to prayer, to the examination of his own life, to the purification of memory, to the openness of charity.

The father of spiritual ecumenism, Paul Couturier, spoke in

this regard of an "invisible cloister" which unites within its walls those souls inflamed with love for Christ and his Church. I am convinced that if more and more people unite themselves interiorly to the Lord's prayer "that all may be one" (Jn 17:21), then this prayer, made in the Name of Jesus, will not go unheard (cf. Jn 14:13; 15:7, 16, etc.).

With the help that comes from on high, we will also find practical solutions to the different questions which remain open, and in the end our desire for unity will come to fulfillment, whenever and however the Lord wills.

Now let us all go along this path in the awareness that walking together is a form of unity. Let us thank God for this and pray that he will continue to guide us all.

Concluding Talks

APOSTOLIC JOURNEY TO COLOGNE
ON THE OCCASION OF
THE TWENTIETH WORLD YOUTH DAY

MEETING WITH THE GERMAN BISHOPS

ADDRESS OF HIS HOLINESS POPE BENEDICT XVI

COLOGNE—ARCHBISHOP'S HOUSE / SUNDAY, 21 AUGUST 2005

Venerable and Dear Brothers,

First of all, I would like to express my great happiness at once again having the opportunity to see one another and be together after beautiful and likewise demanding days and, therefore, of having the joy of meeting. Although I am in fact only a former member of the German Bishops' Conference, I still feel bound to you all in a fraternal union that cannot weaken.

I would like next to thank Cardinal Lehmann for his cordial words and emphasize them in the spirit of what I too said today *at the end of this Eucharistic celebration*: that is, I want to express once again the great "thank you" that we all have in our hearts.

We all know that the immense work of preparation, the great things achieved, do not suffice to make all this possible. We know, consequently, that it must necessarily be a gift. Since no one can simply create the enthusiasm of the young, no one can create to last for days this union in faith and in the joy of faith.

Everything, moreover, even the weather, has truly been a gift for which we thank the Lord. We also interpret it as a duty to do our part to ensure that this enthusiasm continues and develops into strength for the life of the Church in our Country.

I would like once again to thank Cardinal Meisner and his collaborators for all their preparatory work. I also want to thank Cardinal Lehmann, his collaborators and all of you, for all the Dioceses have cooperated in the organization of this event. The whole of Germany has offered hospitality to the guests and has set out with Our Lady and the Cross; it has thus been able to receive this gift.

I am deeply grateful for this statue that still needs a little time, so to speak, to acquire its definitive form. Yet I find it very beautiful that Saint Boniface will also be in my house and will thus visibly express to me too what he held particularly dear: the union between the Church in Germany and in Rome. Just as he led the Church in Germany to unity with the Successor of Peter, he is also guiding me to lasting fraternal communion with the Bishops of Germany, with the Church in Germany.

The Holy Father John Paul II, the brilliant founder of the *World Youth Days*—an insight that I consider an inspiration— has shown that both parties give and receive. Not only have we done our part in the best possible way, but the young people, with their questions, their hope, their joy in faith, their enthusiasm in renewing the Church, have given something to us.

Let us give thanks for this reciprocity and let us hope that it will endure, that is, that the young people with their questions, faith and joy in faith will continue to challenge us to get the better of our faint-heartedness and weariness and urge us, in turn, with the experience of the faith that is given to us, with the experience of pastoral ministry, with the grace of the Sacrament in which we find ourselves, to point out the way to them, so that their enthusiasm may be properly directed. Just as a spring must be channeled so that its waters may be useful, this ever new enthusiasm must likewise be, as it were, molded into its ecclesial form.

Here in Germany we are accustomed primarily, and I as a Professor in particular, to see especially the problems. However, I believe we should admit that all this has been possible because in Germany, despite all the Church's problems, despite all possible questionable things, a living Church truly exists.

She is a Church with many positive aspects in which so many people are ready to work hard for their own faith and to use their free time, even giving money and some of their possessions simply to contribute to her with their own lives. It seems to me that this has become newly visible to us.

How many people in Germany, in spite of all the difficulties we complain about, are still believers today, constitute a living Church and, hence, make it possible for an event like World Youth Day to have its own context, its own *humus*, in which to grow and take shape!

I believe we must remember the many priests, Religious and lay people who, faithful to their service, work in difficult pastoral conditions. And there is no need for me to emphasize the generosity of German Catholics, truly well known throughout the world; it is not only a material generosity, since there are many German *Fidei donum* priests.

I see it during the *Ad limina* visits: German priests are working, even in Papua New Guinea, the Solomon Islands and regions beyond the wildest imagination, scattering the seed of the Word, identifying with people. Thus, they imbue this threatened world, invaded by so many negative things from the West, with the great power of faith and, with it, all that is positive in what we are given.

Misereor, Adveniat, Missio, Renovabis as well as the diocesan and parish branches of *Caritas* do an enormous amount of work. Then the educational work of Catholic schools and other Catholic institutions and organizations for youth is equally vast. In saying this, I do not intend to be exhaustive about everything positive there is to say, but merely to mention it to you so that these aspects are not forgotten and will always inspire courage and joy.

Besides the positive aspects that I believe are important not to forget and for which it is always necessary to be grateful, we also have to admit that on the face of the universal Church and also on that of the Church in Germany there are unfortunately also wrinkles and shadows that obscure her splendor. We should lovingly keep these before us, too, at this moment of festivity and thanksgiving.

We know that secularism and dechristianization are gaining ground, that relativism is growing and that the influence of Catholic ethics and morals is in constant decline. Many people abandon the Church or, if they stay, accept only a part of Catholic teaching, picking and choosing between only certain aspects of Christianity.

The religious situation in the East continues to be worrying. Here, as we know, the majority of the population is not baptized, has no contact with the Church and has often not even heard of either Christ or the Church. We should recognize these realities as challenges.

Dear Brothers, as you yourselves said in your Pastoral Letter of 21 September 2004, on the occasion of the Jubilee of Saint Boniface: "We have become a mission land." This is true for large parts of Germany.

I therefore believe that throughout Europe, and likewise in France, Spain and elsewhere, we should give serious thought as to how to achieve a true evangelization in this day and age, not only a new evangelization, but often a true and proper first evangelization.

People do not know God, they do not know Christ. There is a new form of paganism, and it is not enough for us to strive to preserve the existing flock, although this is very important: we must ask the important question: What really is life?

I believe we must all try together to find new ways of bringing the Gospel to the contemporary world, of proclaiming Christ anew and of implanting the faith.

This scene that the World Youth Day is unfolding before us and that I have described with only a few brief comments invites us to turn our gaze to the future. For the Church and especially for us Pastors, for parents and for educators, young people constitute a living appeal to faith.

I would like to say once again that in my opinion Pope John Paul II was tremendously inspired in choosing for this *World*

Youth Day the motto: *"We have come to worship him"* (Mt 2:2). We are often so oppressed, understandably oppressed, by the immense social needs of the world and by all the organizational and structural problems that exist that we set aside worship as something for later. Father Delp once said that nothing is more important than worship. He said so in the context of his time, when it was evident that to destroy worship, destroyed man.

Nonetheless, in our new context in which worship, and thus also the face of human dignity, has been lost, it is once again up to us to understand the priority of worship. We must make youth, ourselves and our communities aware of the fact that it is not a luxury of our confused epoch that we cannot permit ourselves but a priority. Wherever worship is no longer, wherever it is not a priority to pay honor to God, human realities can make no headway.

We must therefore endeavor to make the face of Christ visible, the face of the living God, so that like the Magi we may spontaneously fall to our knees and adore him. Two things certainly happened in the Magi: first they sought; then they found and worshipped him.

Today, many people are searching. We too are searching. Basically, in a different dialectic, both these things must always exist within us. We must respect man's search. We must support it and make him feel that faith is not merely a dogmatism complete in itself that puts an end to seeking, that extinguishes man's great thirst, but that it directs the great pilgrimage towards the infinite; we, as believers, are always simultaneously seekers and finders.

In his Commentary on the Psalms, Saint Augustine interprets so splendidly the expression *"Quaerite faciem eius semper"*, "constantly seek his face", that ever since my student days his words have lived on in my heart. This is true not only for this life, but for eternity; his face must be ceaselessly rediscovered. The more deeply we penetrate the splendor of divine love, the greater will be our discoveries and the more beautiful it will be to travel on and to know that our seeking has no end and, hence, finding has no end, and therefore eternity is at the same time the joy of seeking and finding.

We must support people in their search as fellow-seekers, and at the same time we must also give them the certainty that God has found us and, consequently, that we can find him. We want to be a Church open to the future, rich in promises for the new generations.

It is not a matter of pandering to youth, which is basically ridiculous, but of a true youthfulness that flows from the well-springs of eternity, that is ever new, that derives from the transparency of Christ in his Church: this is how he gives us the light to continue. In this light we can find the courage to face confidently the most difficult questions asked in the Church in Germany today.

As I have already said, on the one hand, we must accept the challenges of youth, but on the other, we in turn must inculcate in young people patience, without which nothing can be found; we must teach them discernment, a healthy realism, the capacity to be decisive. A Head of State who paid me a visit recently told me that his main concern was the widespread inability to make definitive decisions for fear of losing personal freedom.

In fact, man becomes free when he binds himself, when he finds roots, for it is then that he can grow and mature. We must teach patience, discernment, realism, but without false compromises, so as not to water down the Gospel!

The experience of these past twenty years has taught us that every World Youth Day is in a certain sense a new beginning for the pastoral care of young people in the country that hosts it. Preparing for the event mobilizes people and resources. We have seen it right here in Germany: how a true "mobilization" has pervaded the Country, prompting a surge of energy.

Lastly, the celebration itself brings a gust of enthusiasm that must be sustained and, so to speak, rendered definitive. This enormous potential energy can further increase, spreading across the territory. I am thinking of the parishes, associations and movements. I am thinking of the priests, Religious, catechists and animators involved with young people. I believe that in Germany the large number of people involved in this event is well known. I am praying that each one of those who collaborated may genuinely grow in love for Christ and for the Church, and I encourage them all to carry on their pastoral work among the new generations together, with a renewed spirit of service. We must relearn willingness to serve, and transmit it.

The majority of young Germans live in comfortable social and financial conditions. Yet we know well that difficult situations are not lacking.

In all social strata, especially those that are better off, the number of young people from broken families is on the rise. Unfortunately, unemployment among young people in Germany has increased.

Moreover, many young men and women are bewildered and have no real answers to their questions about the meaning of life and death, about their present and their future. Many of the ideas put forward by modern society lead nowhere, and, unfortunately, very many young people end in the quicksand of alcohol and drugs or in the clutches of extremist groups.

Some young Germans, especially in the East, have never become personally acquainted with the Good News of Jesus Christ. Even in the traditionally Catholic regions, the teaching of religion and catechesis do not always manage to forge lasting bonds between young people and the Church community.

For this reason you are all committed together—I know it— to seeking new ways to reach out to young people, and the World Youth Days have been—as Pope John Paul II used to say—a sort of "laboratory" for this.

I think we are all reflecting—and in the other Western countries it is just the same—on how to make catechesis more effective. I read in the *HERDER-Korrespondenz* that you have published a new catechetical document that I have unfortunately not yet had an opportunity to see, but I am grateful to note that you are taking this problem to heart.

Indeed, it is worrying to us all that despite the age-old teaching of religion, the knowledge of religion is meager, and many people often do not even know the most basic, elementary things. What can we do?

I do not know. Perhaps on the one hand, heathens should have access to a sort of pre-catechesis that opens them to the faith—and this is also the content of many catechetical endeavors—but on the other, it is always necessary to have the courage to transmit the mystery itself, in its beauty and greatness, and pave the way to the impulse to contemplate, love and recognize it: ah, this is it!

Today, in *my Homily* I noted that Pope John Paul II gave us two exceptional instruments: the *Catechism of the Catholic Church* and its *Compendium*, which he also wanted. We made sure that the German translation was ready for World Youth Day. In Italy, half a million copies have already been sold. It is on sale at the newsstands and rouses peoples' curiosity. What is in it? What does the Catholic Church say?

I believe we too must have the courage to sustain this curiosity and to attempt to make these books that represent the content of the mystery a part of catechesis, so that by increasing the knowledge of our faith the joy that stems from it will also increase.

I have two other aspects very much at heart. One is the pastoral care of vocations.

I feel that the recitation of Vespers in the Church of Saint Pantaleon has also given us the courage to help young people and to do so in the right way, so that the Lord's call may reach them and they ask themselves: "Does he want me?" and so that once again the willingness to be called and to hear such a call may increase.

The other aspect very dear to me is the pastoral care of families. We see the threat to families; in the meantime even lay bodies recognize how important it is that the family live as the primary cell of society, that children be able to grow in an atmosphere of communion between the generations, so that continuity between the present, past and future will endure and that the continuity of values will be lasting: this is what makes it possible to build communion in a country.

I wanted to deal precisely with these three aspects: catechesis, the pastoral care of vocations and the pastoral care of families.

As we have seen, associations and movements, which are undoubtedly a source of enrichment, play an important role in the world of youth. The Church must make the most of these realities, and at the same time she must guide them with pastoral wisdom, so that with the variety of their different gifts they may contribute in the best possible way to building up the community without ever entering into competition—each one building, so to speak, its own little church—but respecting one another and working together for the one Church—for the one parish as the local Church—to awaken in young people the joy of faith, love for the Church and passion for the Kingdom of God.

I think that precisely this is another important aspect: this authentic communion on the one hand between the various movements whose forms of exclusivism should be eliminated, and on the other, between the local Churches and the movements, so that the local Churches recognize this particularity, which seems strange to many, and welcome it in itself as a treasure, understanding that in the Church there are many ways and that all together they converge in a symphony of faith. The local Churches and movements are not in opposition to one another, but constitute the living structure of the Church.

Dear Brothers, please God, there will be other occasions on which to go deeply into the issues that challenge our common pastoral solicitude. This time I wanted, very briefly and not exhaustively, of course, to convey the message that the great pilgrimage of young people has left us. It seems to me that at the end of this event, the young people's request to us might be summed up as: "Yes, we came to worship him. We met him.

Now help us to become his disciples and witnesses." It is a demanding appeal, but especially comforting to a Pastor's heart.

May the memory of the days spent in Cologne under the banner of hope sustain our common service!

I leave you with my affectionate encouragement, which at the same time is a heartfelt brotherly request: always proceed and work in agreement, on the basis of a communion of which the Eucharist is the summit and the source.

I entrust you all to Mary, the Mother of Christ and of the Church, and I impart my Apostolic Blessing to each one of you and to your communities. Thank you.

APOSTOLIC JOURNEY TO COLOGNE
ON THE OCCASION OF
THE TWENTIETH WORLD YOUTH DAY

DEPARTURE CEREMONY

ADDRESS OF HIS HOLINESS POPE BENEDICT XVI

COLOGNE AIRPORT / SUNDAY, 21 AUGUST 2005

Distinguished Mr. President,
Dear Young Friends,
Ladies and Gentlemen,

At the conclusion of this, *my first Visit to Germany* as the Bishop of Rome and the Successor of Peter, I must express once again my heartfelt gratitude for the welcome given to me, to my collaborators and especially to the many young people who came to Cologne from every continent for this *World Youth Day.*

The Lord has called me to succeed our beloved Pope John Paul II, whose inspired idea it was to initiate the series of *World Youth Days.* I have taken up this legacy with awe and also with joy, and I give thanks to God for giving me the opportunity to experience in the company of so many young people this further step along their spiritual pilgrimage from continent to continent, following the Cross of Christ.

I am grateful to all those who have so effectively ensured that every phase of this extraordinary gathering could take place in an orderly and serene fashion. These days spent together have given many young men and women from the whole world the opportunity to become better acquainted with Germany.

We are all well aware of the evil that emerged from our Homeland during the twentieth century, and we acknowledge it with shame and suffering.

During these days, thanks be to God, it has become quite evident that there was and is another Germany, a Land of singular human, cultural and spiritual resources. I hope and pray that these resources, thanks, not least, to the events of recent days, may once more spread throughout the world!

Now young people from all over the world can return home enriched by their contacts and their experiences of dialogue and fellowship in the different regions of our Homeland. I am certain that their stay, marked by their youthful enthusiasm, will remain as a pleasant memory with the people who have offered them such generous hospitality, and that it will also be a sign of hope for Germany.

Indeed, one can say that during these days Germany has been the center of the Catholic world.

Young people from every continent and culture, gathered in faith around their Pastors and the Successor of Peter, have shown us a young Church, one that seeks with imagination and courage to shape the face of a more just and generous humanity.

Following the example of the Magi, these young men and women set out to encounter Christ, in accordance with the theme of this World Youth Day. Now they are returning to their own regions and cities to testify to the light, the beauty and the power of the Gospel which they have experienced anew.

Before leaving, I must also express thanks to all who have opened their hearts and their homes to the countless young pilgrims. I am grateful to the Government Authorities, to the political leaders and the various civil and military departments, as well as the security services and the many volunteer organizations which have put so much effort into the preparation and realization of each of the initiatives and events of this World Youth Day.

A special word of thanks goes to all who planned the moments of prayer and reflection, as well as the liturgical celebrations, eloquent examples of the joyful vitality of the faith that animates the younger generation in our time.

I would also like to express my gratitude to the leaders of other Churches and Ecclesial Communities and to the representatives of other religions who wished to be present at this important meeting. I express my hope that we can strengthen our common commitment to train the younger generation in the human and spiritual values which are indispensable for building a future of true freedom and peace.

My deep gratitude goes to Cardinal Joachim Meisner, Archbishop of Cologne, the Diocese that hosted this international meeting; to the Bishops of Germany, led by the President of the Bishops' Conference, Cardinal Karl Lehmann; to the priests; to men and women Religious; and to the parish communities, lay associations and movements who have devoted such energy to helping the young people present to reap the spiritual fruits of their stay.

I offer a special word of thanks to the young people from Germany, who in a variety of ways have helped to welcome other young people and to share with them moments of faith that have been truly memorable. I hope that this event will remain impressed on the life of Germany's Catholics and will be an incentive for a renewed spiritual and apostolic outreach!

May the Gospel be received in its integrity and witnessed with profound conviction by all Christ's disciples, so that it becomes a source of authentic renewal for all of German society, thanks also to dialogue with the different Christian communities and the followers of other religions.

Finally, my respectful and cordial greetings go to the political, civil and diplomatic Authorities present at this Departure Ceremony. In particular, I thank you, Mr. President, for your courtesy in desiring to welcome me in person at the beginning of my Visit and for having desired to be present once again at my Farewell Ceremony. Thank you with all my heart!

Through you, I thank the Government Members and the entire German People, whose numerous representatives have been so cordial in these intense hours of communion.

Filled with the emotions and memories of these days, I now return to Rome. Upon all of you I invoke God's abundant Blessings for a future of serene prosperity, harmony and peace.

BENEDICT XVI

GENERAL AUDIENCE

WEDNESDAY, 24 AUGUST 2005

WORLD YOUTH DAY IN COLOGNE

Dear Brothers and Sisters,

Just as beloved John Paul II used to do after every Apostolic Pilgrimage, today I too would like to run through with you the days I spent in Cologne for *World Youth Day*.

Divine Providence determined that the destination of *my first Apostolic Journey* outside Italy be in my native Country and that it take place on the occasion of the great meeting of the world's young people, twenty years after the establishment of World Youth Day, desired with prophetic insight by my unforgettable Predecessor. After my return, I thank God from the bottom of my heart for the gift of this pilgrimage, of which I shall cherish beloved memories.

We all felt that it was a gift of God. Of course, many people worked together, but in the end the grace of this event was a gift from on high, from the Lord.

At the same time, I address my thanks to all those who prepared and organized every phase of the meeting with loving commitment: in the first place, Cardinal Joachim Meisner, Archbishop of Cologne; Cardinal Karl Lehmann, President of the Bishops' Conference; and *the Bishops of Germany, to whom I spoke at the very end of my Visit.*

I would then like once again to thank the Authorities, organizers and volunteers who made their contribution. I am also grateful to the people and communities in every part of the world who supported it with their prayers, and to the sick, who offered up their sufferings for the spiritual success of this important appointment.

My spiritual embrace of the young participants of World Youth Day began with *my arrival at the Cologne/Bonn Airport* and continued, ever more filled with emotion, as we sailed down the Rhine from the Rodenkirchenerbrücke Wharf to Cologne, escorted by five other boats representing the five continents.

Then there was an evocative pause at the Poller Rhein-wiesen Wharf, where thousands and thousands of young people were already waiting. With them I had my first official Meeting, appropriately called the "*Welcome Celebration*" and whose motto was the Magi's question: "Where is the newborn King of the Jews?" (Mt 2:2). The Magi themselves were the "guides" of those young pilgrims bound for Christ, adorers of the mystery of his presence in the Eucharist.

How significant it is that all this has occurred while we are on our way towards the conclusion of the *Year of the Eucharist*, desired by John Paul II! "*We have come to worship him*": the theme of the Meeting invited everyone to follow the Wise Men in spirit and with them to make an inner journey of conversion to Emmanuel, God-with-us, in order to know him, encounter him and worship him, and after meeting and adoring him, to set out anew, bearing his light and his joy in our hearts, in our innermost depths.

In Cologne, the young people had several opportunities to examine these important spiritual topics deeply; they felt impelled by the Holy Spirit to be enthusiastic and consistent witnesses of Christ, who promised to remain truly present among us in the Eucharist until the end of the world.

I am thinking back to the various moments that I had the joy of spending with them, especially *the Saturday Vigil* and *the Concluding Celebration on Sunday*. Millions of other young people from every corner of the earth joined us in these vivid expressions of faith, thanks to the providential radio and television link-ups.

However, I would like here to recall a special Meeting, *my encounter with the seminarians*, young men called to a more radical and personal following of Christ, Teacher and Pastor. I wanted a specific moment to be devoted to them, also to highlight the vocational dimension typical of *World Youth Days*. In the past twenty years, many vocations to the priesthood and consecrated life have been born precisely during the World Youth Days, privileged occasions when the Holy Spirit makes his call forcefully heard.

The *Ecumenical Meeting with representatives of the other Churches and Ecclesial Communities* fitted in very well with the context of the Cologne Day, rich in hope. Germany's role in ecumenical dialogue is important, both because of the sad history of divisions and because of its important role in the journey of reconciliation.

I hope that dialogue, as a reciprocal exchange of gifts and not only of words, will also help increase and develop that orderly and harmonious "symphony" which is Catholic unity. In this perspective, the World Youth Days are an effective ecumenical "workshop".

And how can we fail to relive with emotion *the visit to the Synagogue of Cologne*, the home of the oldest Jewish Community in Germany? With my Jewish brothers and sisters I commemorated the Shoah and the sixtieth anniversary of the liberation of the Nazi concentration camps.

This year is also the fortieth anniversary of the conciliar Declaration *Nostra Aetate*, which has ushered in a new season of dialogue and spiritual solidarity between Jews and Christians, as well as esteem for the other great religious traditions. Islam occupies a special place among them. Its followers worship the same God and willingly refer to the Patriarch Abraham. That is why *I wanted to meet the representatives of some Muslim Communities*, to whom I expressed the hopes and worries of the rough time in history that we are living through, in the hope that fanaticism and violence will be uprooted and that we will always be able to work together to defend human dignity and protect the fundamental rights of men and women.

Dear brothers and sisters from the heart of the "old" Europe, which unfortunately experienced in the past century horrendous conflicts and inhuman regimes, the young people have relaunched for the humanity of our time the message of hope that does not disappoint, for it is based on the Word of God made flesh in Jesus Christ, who died and rose for our salvation.

In Cologne, the young people encountered and adored Emmanuel, God-with-us, in the mystery of the Eucharist, and they came to understand better that the Church is the great family through which God creates a space of communion and unity between every continent, culture and race, a family vaster than the world that knows limits and boundaries; a "great band of pilgrims", so to speak, who walk together with Christ, guided by him, the bright star that illumines history.

Jesus makes himself our traveling companion in the Eucharist, and the Eucharist—as I said in my Homily at the concluding celebration, borrowing from physics a well-known image—induces "nuclear fission" into the very heart of being (*Homily, Holy Mass, Marienfeld Esplanade, Cologne, 21 August 2005; L'Osservatore Romano* English edition, 24 August 2005, p. 11). Only this innermost explosion of good that overcomes evil can give life to other transformations that are necessary to change the world.

May Jesus, the face of the merciful Lord for every person, continue to light our way, like the star that guided the Magi, and fill us with his joy.

Let us pray, therefore, that the young people of Cologne will take home with them, within them, the light of Christ, which is truth and love, and spread it everywhere. I am confident that through the power of the Holy Spirit and the motherly assistance of the Virgin Mary, we will see a great springtime of hope in Germany, in Europe and throughout the world.